making maths add up

Large print edition

Number, Addition & Place Value!

Book 1

"Finally, a book that the kids like. It's very visual and caters to different levels in the class. Excellent!"   Helen. I (Teacher)

"I love all the pictures like Barry and Doris! They're so funny."   Mae W.

"As a father, I love finding resources that help me support my son's education. This book has given our learning journey some much needed structure."
            Ben A. (Father)

"It's very colourful and easy to understand."   David. S.

Copyright © Maggie Tu 2023

ISBN 978-1-7385926-2-3

Published by Piwaiwaka Press

This book is copyright. Except for the purposes of fair review, no part may be stored or transmitted in any form or by any other means, electronic or mechanical, including recording or storage in any information retrieval system, without permission in writing from the publishers.

Cover by Maggie Tu.

Illustrations on pages 80, 81, 83, 89, 159, 160, 161, 162 by April Hendry. All other illustrations by Maggie Tu.

Layout by Madden Hay and Maggie Tu.

Contents

Welcome & tips 1

Meet the numbers 2

- ANSWERS: Meet the numbers 12

The number line and tidy numbers 13

- ANSWERS: The number line and tidy numbers 17

Understanding bigger numbers with place value 18

Splitting numbers into their place values 22

- ANSWERS: Splitting numbers into their place values 32

Into the hundreds and thousands 34

- ANSWERS: Into the hundreds and thousands 44

Counting and word problems 46

- ANSWERS: Counting and word problems 51

Algebra 52

- ANSWERS: Algebra 58

Behind the scenes of addition 60

- ANSWERS: Behind the scenes of addition 66

Mastering basic facts for zero to ten 67

- ANSWERS: Mastering basic facts for zero to ten 77

Understanding word problems 80

- ANSWERS: Understanding word problems 84

Pairs to 10 86

- ANSWERS: Pairs to 10 96

Using pairs to 10 for higher additions 100

- ANSWERS: Using pairs to 10 for higher additions 108

Shortcuts for adding 10 (and numbers close to 10) 111

- ANSWERS: Shortcuts for adding 10 (and numbers close to 10) ... 120

Doubles and pairs to 20 123

- ANSWERS: Doubles and pairs to 20 137

Up into the hundreds 146

- ANSWERS: Up into the hundreds 153

A final review 156

Bonus: Solve the word problems 159

- ANSWERS: A final review 163

- ANSWERS: Solve the word problems 166

Welcome! Here are some tips for using this book.

This book teaches you maths in an exciting new way that you can understand and enjoy. Here's how I recommend you use it:

❖ **Go through the book in order.**

This book starts at the beginning of each topic so it might be easier at the start of each chapter and harder at the end. Therefore, you can jump in at the point where you feel you can learn something new. However, if the questions are a teeny bit tricky take the time to get it super smooth before moving on.

❖ **Always, always, ALWAYS check your answers!**

You can check your answers as you go or at the end of each chapter. If you didn't get something right, see if you can work out what you need to do to fix it. Never be afraid of getting a question 'wrong'. Mistakes are the best way to learn!

❖ **Write your own questions.**

I have given you lots of exercises but if you want to practise more questions on a topic, make up your own. It's one thing to solve an equation, but it takes an even deeper level of understanding to be able to create and solve your own equations.

I do hope you discover a new way of working with numbers that inspires you and helps you gain the skills and confidence you need to continue exploring on your own!

Maggie

Meet the numbers!

Numbers are symbols that help us keep track of and represent things. Imagine if we wanted to buy 5 apples from someone, but we didn't have the number 5.

In a world WITHOUT numbers

A few apples, yes, some more, no, no, that's too many, wait ... almost there, yes, perfect, thank you!

In a world WITH numbers:

5 apples please!

And then imagine trying to do things like figuring out if you have enough money to buy a cat or a dog!

So numbers are rather helpful. They save us a lot of time, and help us do some pretty cool things. Every single number is written using a combination of just these digits:

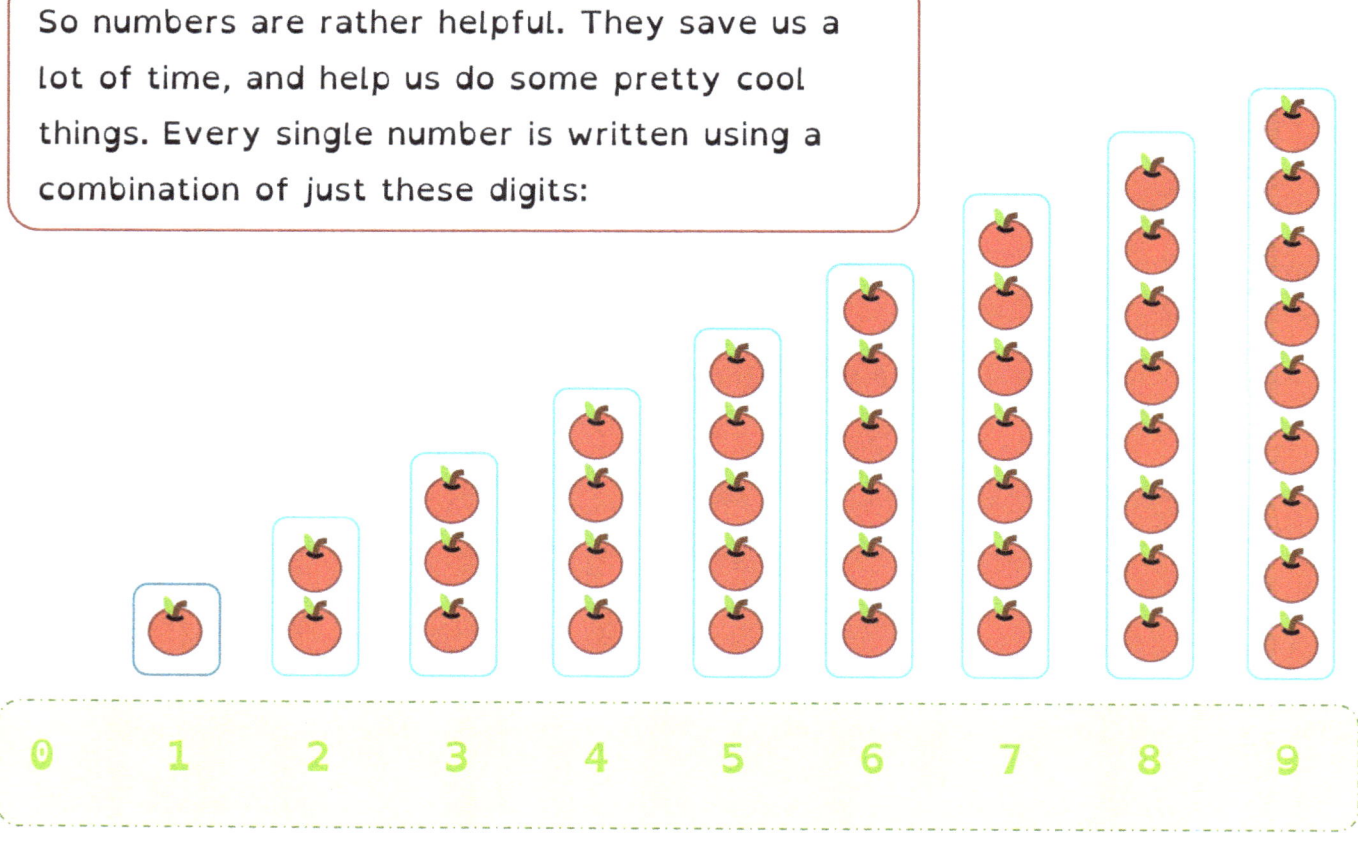

Counting

This is a hundred square. The orange arrows show how the numbers going across are +1, and the green arrows show how those going down are +10.

1	2	3	4	5	6	7	8	9	10
11	12	13	14	15	16	17	18	19	20
21	22	23	24	25	26	27	28	29	30
31	32	33	34	35	36	37	38	39	40
41	42	43	44	45	46	47	48	49	50
51	52	53	54	55	56	57	58	59	60
61	62	63	64	65	66	67	68	69	70
71	72	73	74	75	76	77	78	79	80
81	82	83	84	85	86	87	88	89	90
91	92	93	94	95	96	97	98	99	100

It's a great way to learn how we talk about numbers. Do you see any patterns? Grab some colouring pencils, and colour the numbers on the grid on the next page so each digit from 0 to 9 has a different colour.

For example:

2 –    3 –

6 – orange   7 – blue

9 – red

Colour to your heart's content!

1	2	3	4	5	6	7	8	9	10
11	12	13	14	15	16	17	18	19	20
21	22	23	24	25	26	27	28	29	30
31	32	33	34	35	36	37	38	39	40
41	42	43	44	45	46	47	48	49	50
51	52	53	54	55	56	57	58	59	60
61	62	63	64	65	66	67	68	69	70
71	72	73	74	75	76	77	78	79	80
81	82	83	84	85	86	87	88	89	90
91	92	93	94	95	96	97	98	99	100

Key:

(the colour you're colouring each digit)

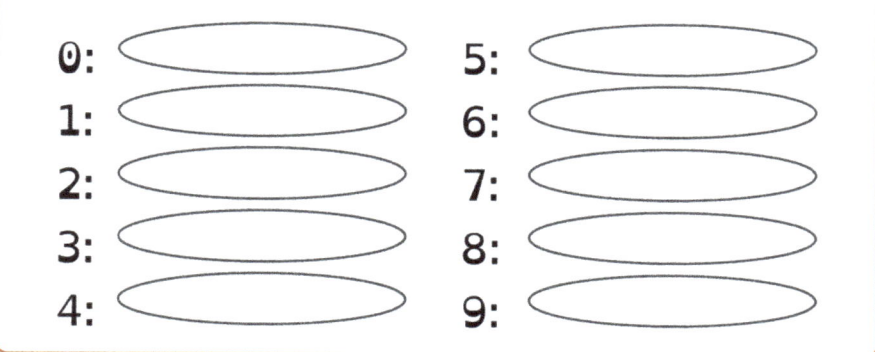

0:
1:
2:
3:
4:
5:
6:
7:
8:
9:

Just so we're clear, counting up a number line (by ones) looks like this:

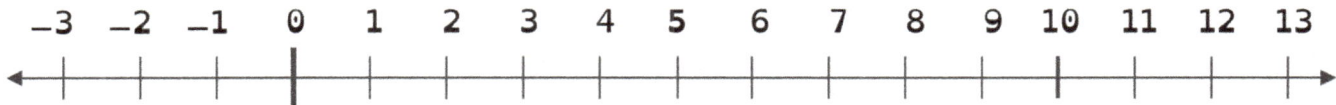

And counting up a hundreds square (by ones) looks like this:

1	2	3	4	5	6	7	8	9	10
11	12	13	14	15	16	17	18	19	20
21	22	23	24	25	26	27	28	29	30
31	32	33	34	35	36	37	38	39	40
41	42	43	44	45	46	47	48	49	50
51	52	53	54	55	56	57	58	59	60
61	62	63	64	65	66	67	68	69	70
71	72	73	74	75	76	77	78	79	80
81	82	83	84	85	86	87	88	89	90
91	92	93	94	95	96	97	98	99	100

8	9	10
18	19	20

If you want to add 10 just slide down a row (anywhere you like).

↓ +10

64	65	66
74	75	76

Take a look at how the pattern continues after 100.
Each coloured row is a group of 10.
This pattern can go on and on forever!

1	2	3	4	5	6	7	8	9	10
11	12	13	14	15	16	17	18	19	20
21	22	23	24	25	26	27	28	29	30
31	32	33	34	35	36	37	38	39	40
41	42	43	44	45	46	47	48	49	50
51	52	53	54	55	56	57	58	59	60
61	62	63	64	65	66	67	68	69	70
71	72	73	74	75	76	77	78	79	80
81	82	83	84	85	86	87	88	89	90
91	92	93	94	95	96	97	98	99	100
101	102	103	104	105	106	107	108	109	110
111	112	113	114	115	116	117	118	119	120
121	122	123	124	125	126	127	128	129	130

1. Now that you know the pattern, fill in the missing numbers!

1		3	4	5	6	7	8	9	10
11	12	13	14	15	16		18	19	20
21	22	23	24		26	27	28	29	30
31	32		34	35	36	37	38	39	
41	42	43		45	46	47		49	50
51	52	53	54		56	57	58	59	60
61	62	63		65	66	67	68	69	70
71	72	73	74	75	76	77	78	79	
	82	83	84	85		87	88	89	90
91	92		94	95	96	97	98		100

2. Now, fill in the missing numbers above a hundred.

101		103	104	105	106		108	109	110
111	112	113		115	116	117	118	119	
	122	123	124	125	126	127		129	130

3. As the pattern is always the same, you can now fill in these squares.

a)

101	102	103	104	105		107	108	109	110
111	112		114	115	116	117	118		120
121	122	123	124	125	126	127		129	130
131	132	133	134	135	136	137	138	139	140
	142	143	144		146	147	148	149	150
151	152	153	154	155	156	157	158	159	
	162	163	164	165	166		168	169	170
171	172		174		176	177	178	179	180
181	182	183	184	185	186	187	188	189	190
	192	193	194	195		197	198	199	

b)

201	202	203	204	205	206			209	210
211		213	214		216	217	218	219	220
221	222	223		225	226	227		229	230
231		233	234	235	236	237	238	239	240

4. These squares have larger numbers, but you can still do it! Fill in the missing numbers.

a

241	242	243	244	245	246	247	248	249	
251	252	253	254		256	257	258	259	260
261		263	264	265	266	267		269	270
271	272	273	274	275	276	277	278	279	280
281	282	283	284	285		287	288	289	
291	292		294	295	296	297	298	299	300

b

431	432	433	434	435	436	437	438	439	440
441		443	444	445	446	447		449	450
451	452	453	454	455	456	457	458		460
461	462	463	464		466	467	468	469	470
	472	473	474	475	476	477	478	479	480
481	482	483	484	485	486	487		489	490
491	492	493		495	496	497	498	499	500

5. Fill in the missing numbers for the 500s and 800s.

a)

501	502	503	504	505	506	507	508	509	510
511		513	514	515	516	517		519	520
521	522	523	524	525		527	528	529	
	532	533	534	535	536	537	538	539	540
541	542	543	544	545	546	547	548		550
551	552	553		555	556	557	558	559	560
561		563	564	565		567	568	569	

b)

801	802	803	804	805	806		808	809	810
	812	813		815	816	817	818	819	820
821	822	823	824	825	826	827		829	830
831	832	833	834	835	836	837	838	839	840
	842	843		845	846	847	848	849	
851	852	853	854	855		857	858	859	860
861	862	863	864	865	866	867		869	870

6. Here's two last grids. Fill in the missing numbers.

a)

931	932		934	935	936	937		939	940
941	942	943	944		946	947	948	949	
951		953	954	955	956		958	959	960
961	962	963	964	965	966	967	968	969	970
971	972	973		975	976	977	978		980
	982	983	984	985	986		988	989	990
991		993	994	995	996	997	998		1000

b)

1001	1002	1003	1004	1005	1006	1007		1009	1010
1011	1012	1013		1015	1016	1017	1018	1019	1020
	1022	1023	1024	1025	1026		1028	1029	1030
1031	1032	1033	1034	1035	1036	1037	1038	1039	1040
1041	1042	1043	1044		1046	1047	1048	1049	
1051		1052	1054	1055	1056	1057		1059	1060

ANSWERS: Meet the numbers!

Page 7

__1.__ 2, 17, 25, 33, 40, 44, 48, 55, 64, 80, 81, 86, 93, 99

__2.__ 102, 107, 114, 120, 121, 128

Page 8

__3.__
a. 106, 113, 119, 128, 141, 145, 160, 161, 167, 173, 175, 191, 196, 200
b. 207, 208, 212, 215, 224, 228, 232

Page 9

__4.__
a. 250, 255, 262, 268, 286, 290, 293
b. 442, 448, 459, 465, 471, 488, 494

Page 10

__5.__
a. 512, 518, 526, 530, 531, 549, 554, 562, 566, 570
b. 807, 811, 814, 828, 841, 844, 850, 856, 868

Page 11

__6.__
a. 933, 938, 945, 950, 952, 957, 974, 979, 981, 987, 992, 999
b. 1008, 1014, 1021, 1027, 1045, 1050, 1052, 1058

Well done!

The number line and tidy numbers

Below is a number line. As we go to the right, the numbers get bigger.

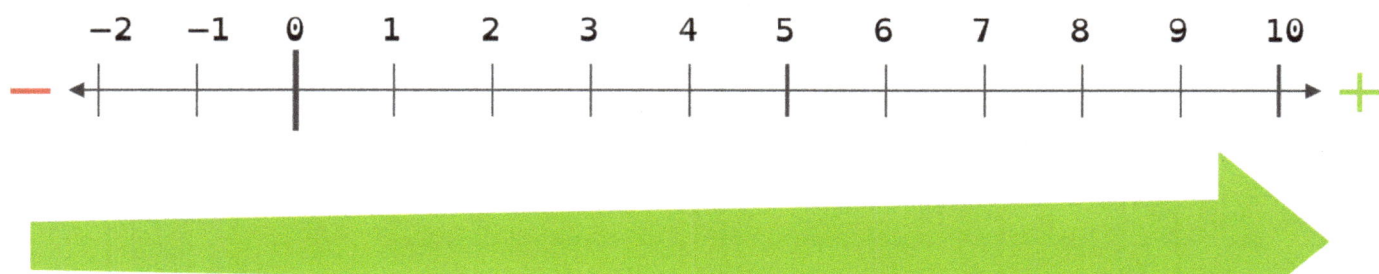

See how 4 is bigger than 3?

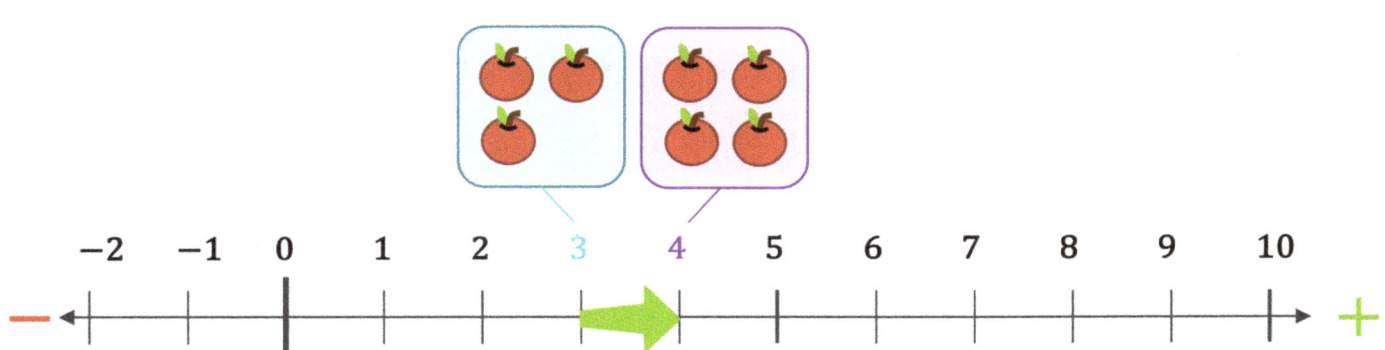

The number 9 is also bigger than 3, but the difference is bigger because it's further along the number line. Numbers close together on the number line have a small difference, while numbers further apart have a larger difference.

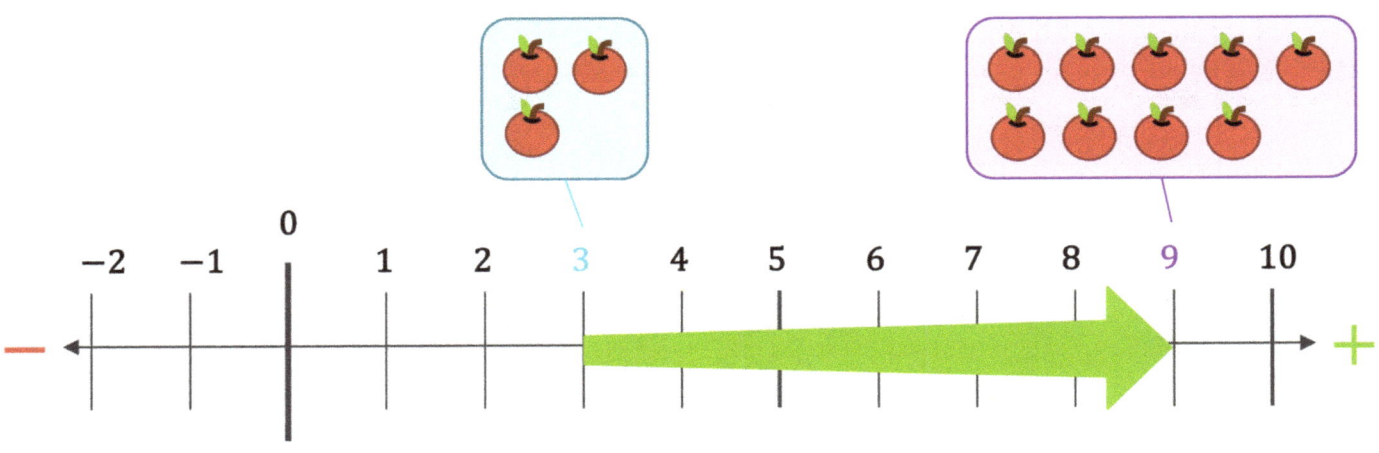

Let's take a closer look at both sides of the number line.

See how the negative side is like a backwards positive side?

1. Can you fill in the missing numbers?

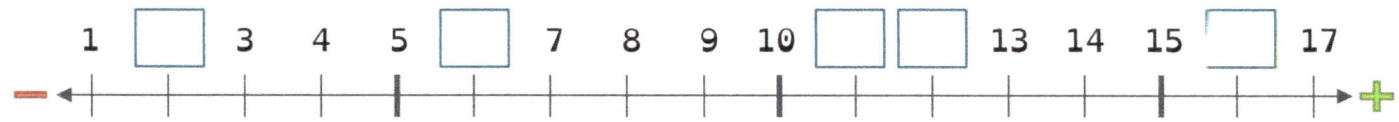

2. And now let's do the negative side.

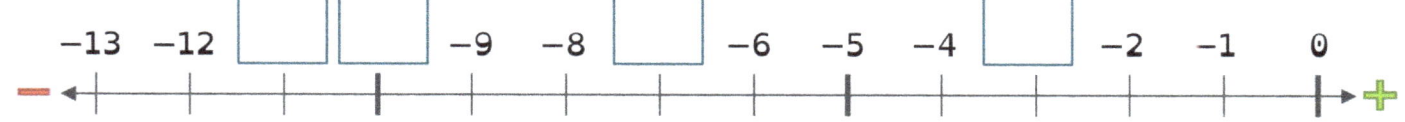

3. Back to positives.

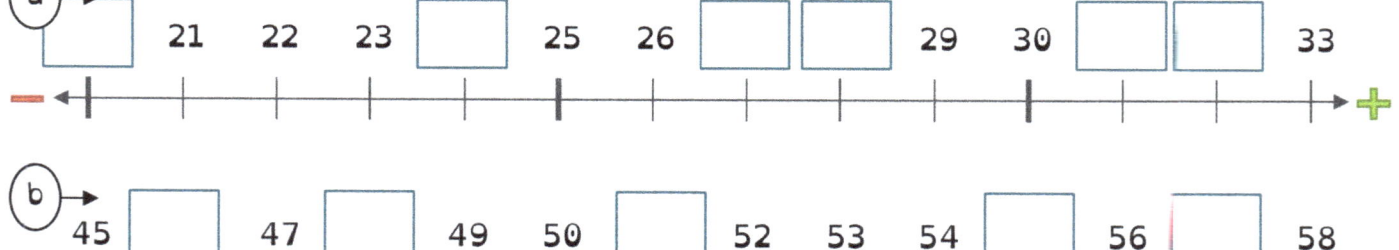

4. Negatives again!

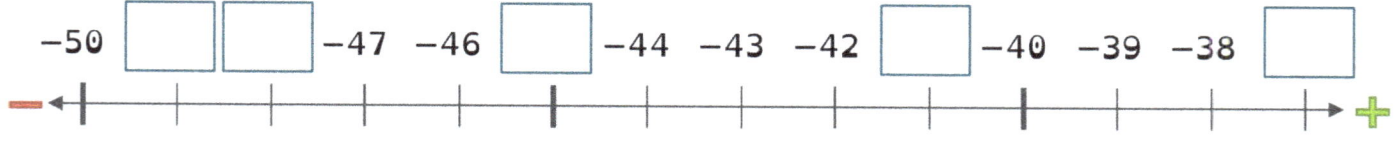

5. And now, fill in the empty boxes on these number lines.

a) [-5] −6 [-5] −4 [-3] −2 −1 0 1 2 3 [4] 5 6 [7]

b) 63 64 [65] 66 67 [68] 69 70 [71] 72 73 74 [75] 76

c) [-40] −39 −38 −37 [-36] −35 [-34] −33 −32 −31 −30 [-29] −28 −27

6. Use the last few pages, or imagine a number line in your head to answer the questions below. Circle the numbers that answer each box's question. Check your answers after you've completed each box.

a) Which of these is BIGGER?

7 or 9?
10 or 5?
12 or 1?
11 or 3?
8 or 2?

b) Which of these is SMALLER?

8 or 5?
9 or 3?
4 or 6?
12 or 2?
5 or 10?

c) Which of these is BIGGER?

−7 or −3?
−8 or −12?
−3 or −10?
−2 or −11?
−5 or −9?

d) Which of these is BIGGER?

67 or 29?
13 or 55?
42 or 18?
11 or 35?
88 or 22?

e) Which of these is SMALLER?

85 or 75?
39 or 93?
42 or 68?
17 or 22?
55 or 18?

f) Which of these is BIGGER?

−75 or −33?
−85 or −12?
−32 or −19?
−21 or −16?
−59 or −92?

Something that you will come across a lot in maths is 'tidy numbers'. They are numbers that are multiples of 10. You can easily tell them apart from other numbers because they always end in a 0!

1	2	3	4	5	6	7	8	9	10
11	12	13	14	15	16	17	18	19	20
21	22	23	24	25	26	27	28	29	30
31	32	33	34	35	36	37	38	39	40
41	42	43	44	45	46	47	48	49	50
51	52	53	54	55	56	57	58	59	60
61	62	63	64	65	66	67	68	69	70
71	72	73	74	75	76	77	78	79	80
81	82	83	84	85	86	87	88	89	90
91	92	93	94	95	96	97	98	99	100

Tidy numbers

These are also tidy numbers:

140   200   1580   76920

7. Circle the tidy numbers below!

23   78   150   305   280

334   60   104   900   30

ANSWERS: The number line and tidy numbers

Page 14

1. 2, 6, 11, 12, 16

2. −11, −10, −7, −3

3.
a. 20, 24, 27, 28, 31, 32
b. 46, 48, 51, 55, 57

4. −49, −48, −45, −41, −37

Page 15

5.
a. −5, −3, 4, 7
b. 65, 68, 71, 75
    c. −40, −36, −34, −29

6.
(answers to be circled going down each box)
a. 9, 10, 12, 11, 8
b. 5, 3, 4, 2, 5
c. −3, −8, −3, −2, −5
d. 67, 55, 42, 88
e. 75, 39, 42, 17, 18
f. −33, −12, −19, −16, −59

Page 16

7. 60, 140, 900, 280, 30 should be circled.

Understanding bigger numbers with place value.

Welcome to place value! There are different positions (spots or places) where digits are written, and that is what gives the number its value. Our numbers work on a base 10 system.

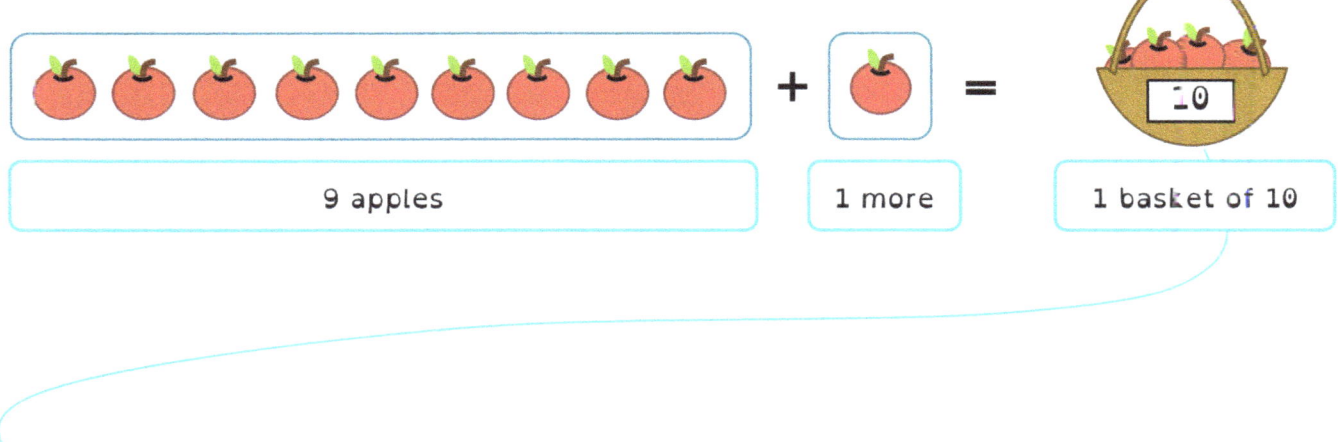

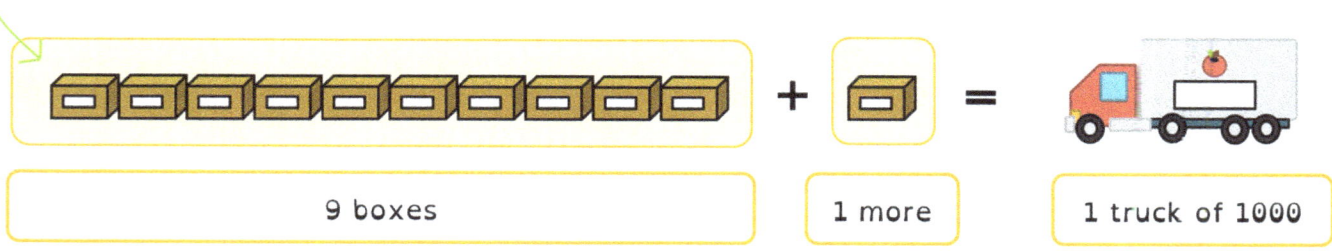

'Base 10' means that every digit's position can only hold 9 groups of something.

As soon as there's any more to make it 10 or bigger, we carry 10 over into a higher position. This makes numbers quick and easy to read.

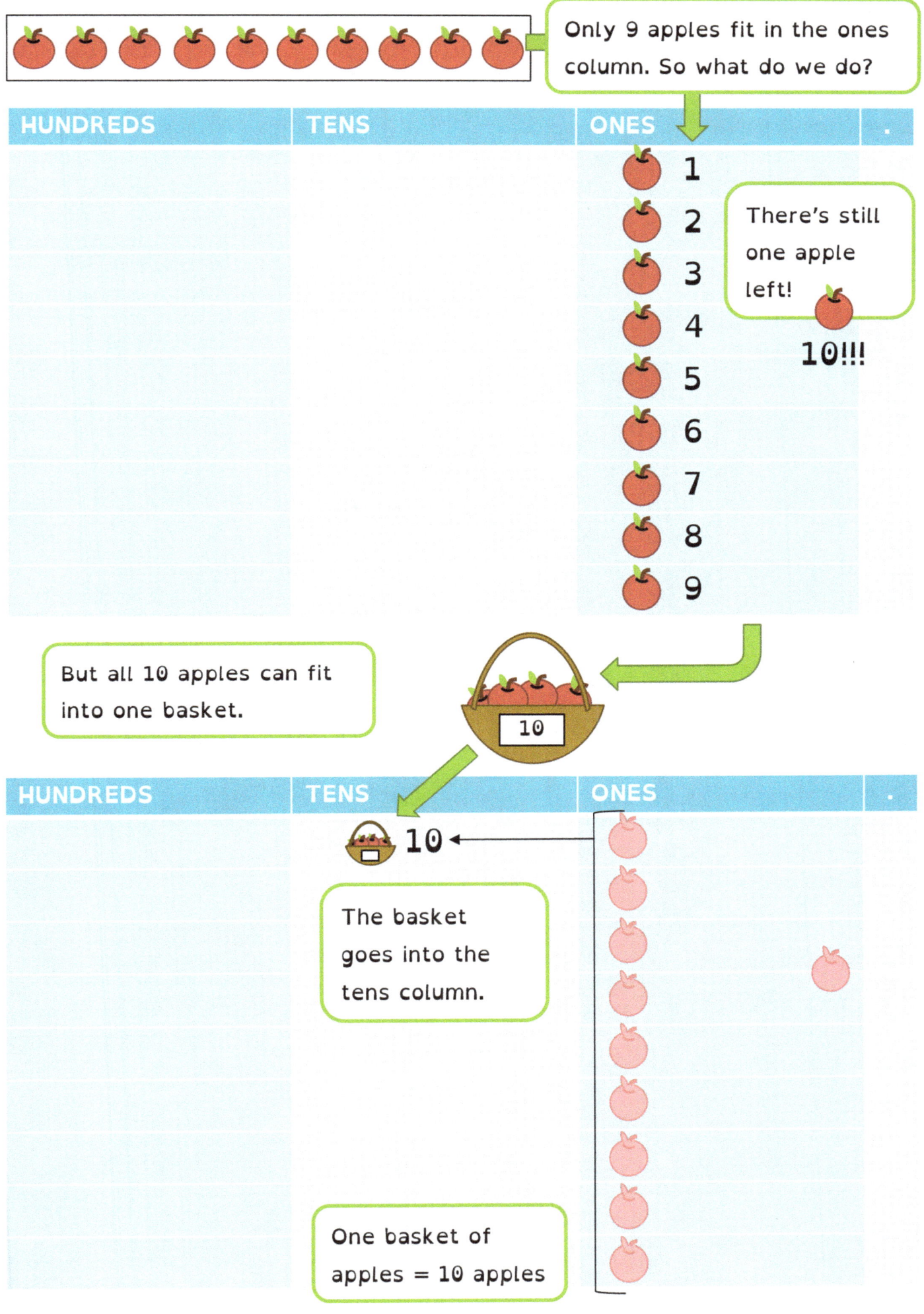

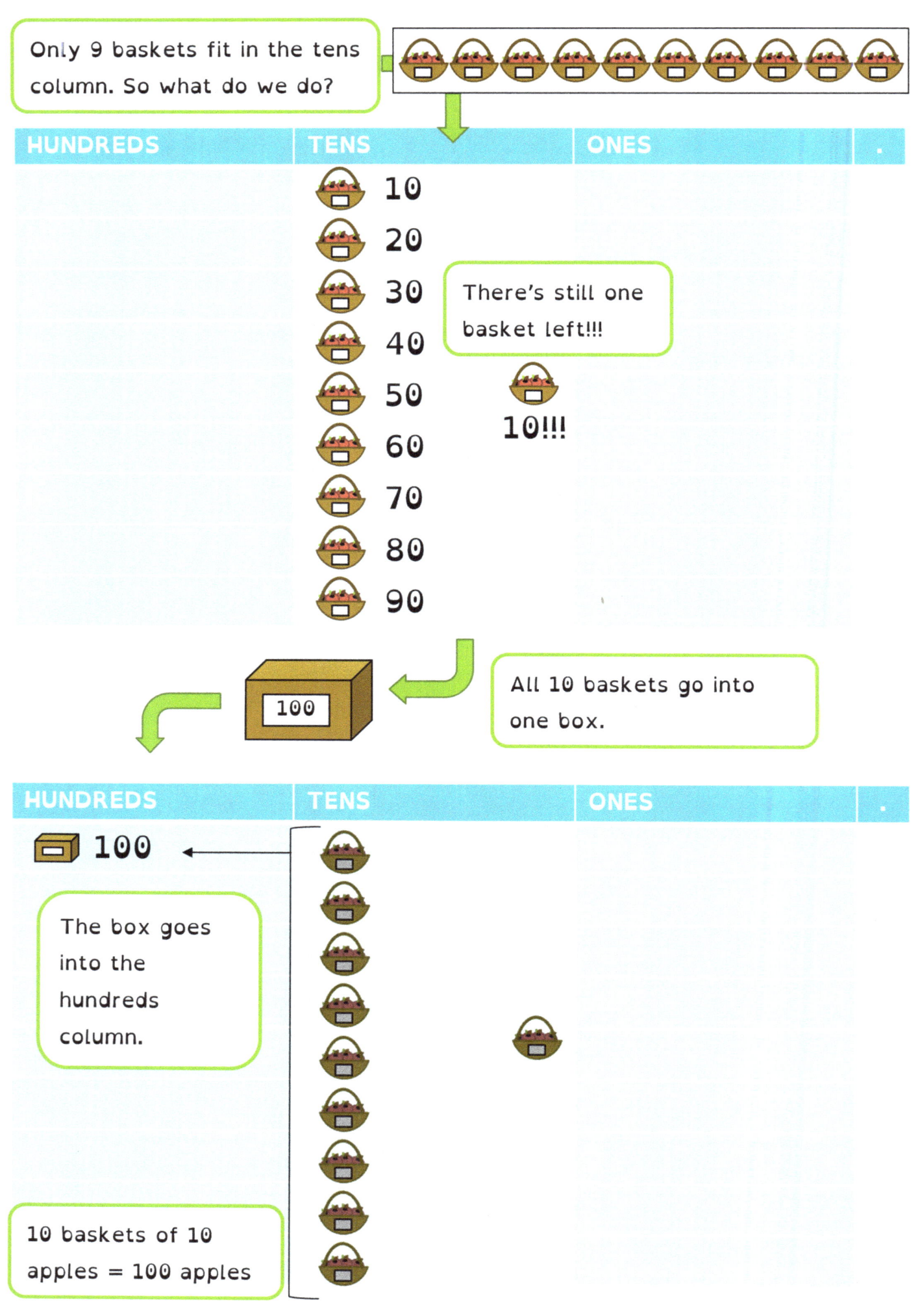

This way of organising numbers makes them easier to read and write. If we represented the number '56' with 56 individual apples that would be a lot of apples. But, place value makes it much tidier.

5 groups of 10 (we put 10 apples into each basket and end up with 5 full baskets)

6 apples that are not enough to fill a basket

This is what all the apples above look like organised in a place value chart.

HUNDREDS	TENS	ONES	.
	10	1	
	20	2	
	30	3	
	40	4	
	50	5	
		6	

And we write the final number like this: 56

| 5 | 6 |

21

Splitting numbers into their place values

29 + 13 = ____

Place value means being able to pull numbers apart while keeping track of their value. It shows how much they represented in the original number. For example, let's take the 29 in the equation above.

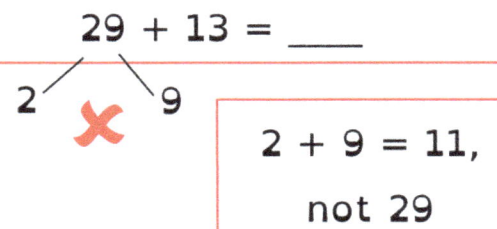

2 + 9 = 11, not 29

This isn't very helpful, because it just tells us that 29 is split into a 2 and a 9.

What we need to do instead is use a zero (0) to act as a placeholder, to tell us how much value the numbers really represent. Here, the 0 in the 20 tells us the 2 is in the tens column.

29 + 13 = ____
20   9 ✓

20 + 9 = 29 ✓

Place values can go as big as you want, but let's start simple. Here's how using just 0 and 5 we can make different numbers and different ways of writing the same number. The secret here is to ignore the number of zeroes BEFORE 5 and to count the number of zeroes AFTER the 5.

5 = 05 = 005 ⇢ Same values

50 = 050 ⇢ Same values

500 ≠ 5000000 ⇢ Not same values

Let's take a closer look at numbers with both tables and apples. If we only had 1 apple, it would go in the ones column like this:

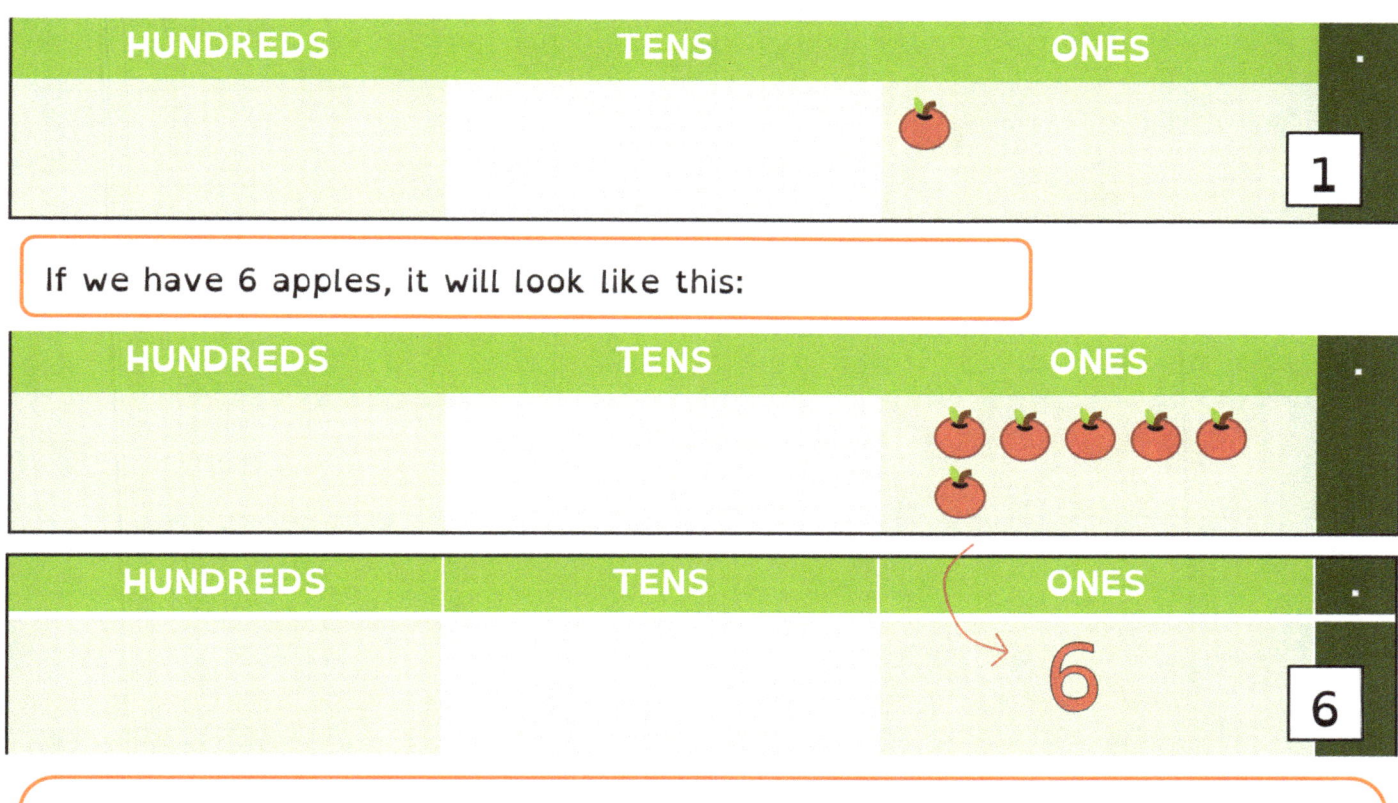

If we have 6 apples, it will look like this:

Once we have 10 apples, we can fill up a basket, which makes them all easier to count and carry. Since a basket has 10 apples, baskets always go in the tens column.

Below is how we group 30 apples.

We don't need a zero before the three.

We do need a zero after the three in the ones column.

Here's a more detailed explanation of what's happening:

There's a zero in the ones column because it's empty.

Here we have 5 baskets, which we can also write as 5 tens.

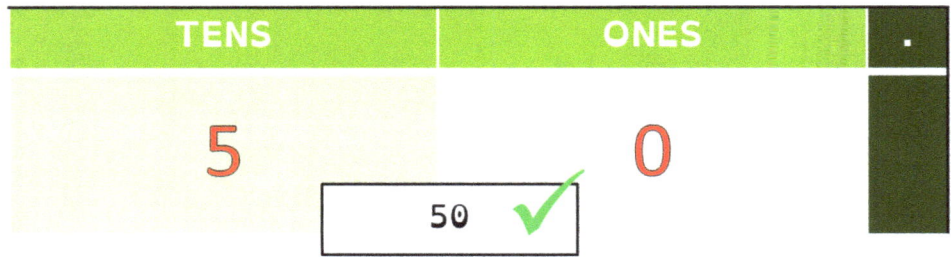

If we didn't write that 0 at the end and left it empty, the 50 would look like 5.

If we have 27 apples, we fit them into 2 baskets of 10 and have 7 apples leftover.

HUNDREDS	TENS	ONES
	🧺🧺	🍎🍎🍎🍎🍎🍎🍎 27

Look at what a difference this makes. It saves us lots of space.

If we show 27 apples without place value, it will look like this:

1. Let's practise with just the tens first. Fill in the gaps.

a)

HUNDREDS	TENS	ONES
	🧺🧺🧺🧺🧺	🚫

HUNDREDS	TENS	ONES
	_____	🚫

_____

b)

HUNDREDS	TENS	ONES
	🧺🧺🧺🧺🧺 🧺🧺🧺🧺	🚫

HUNDREDS	TENS	ONES
	_____	🚫

_____

c)

HUNDREDS	TENS	ONES
	🧺🧺🧺🧺🧺 🧺	🚫

HUNDREDS	TENS	ONES
	_____	🚫

_____

25

2. Same thing here, but write the place values underneath each number too.

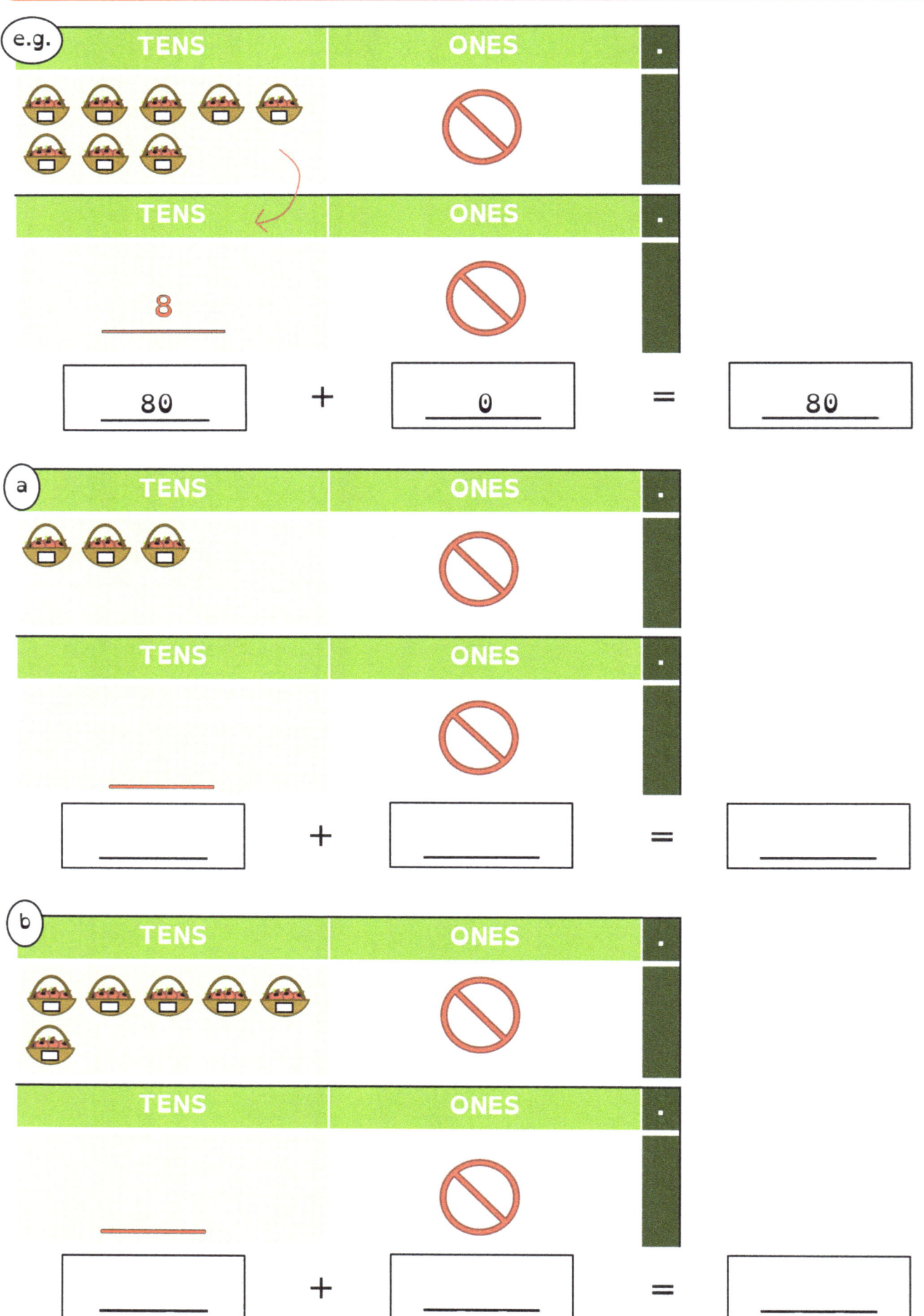

3. Let's try with some apples in the ones column. Fill in the gaps.

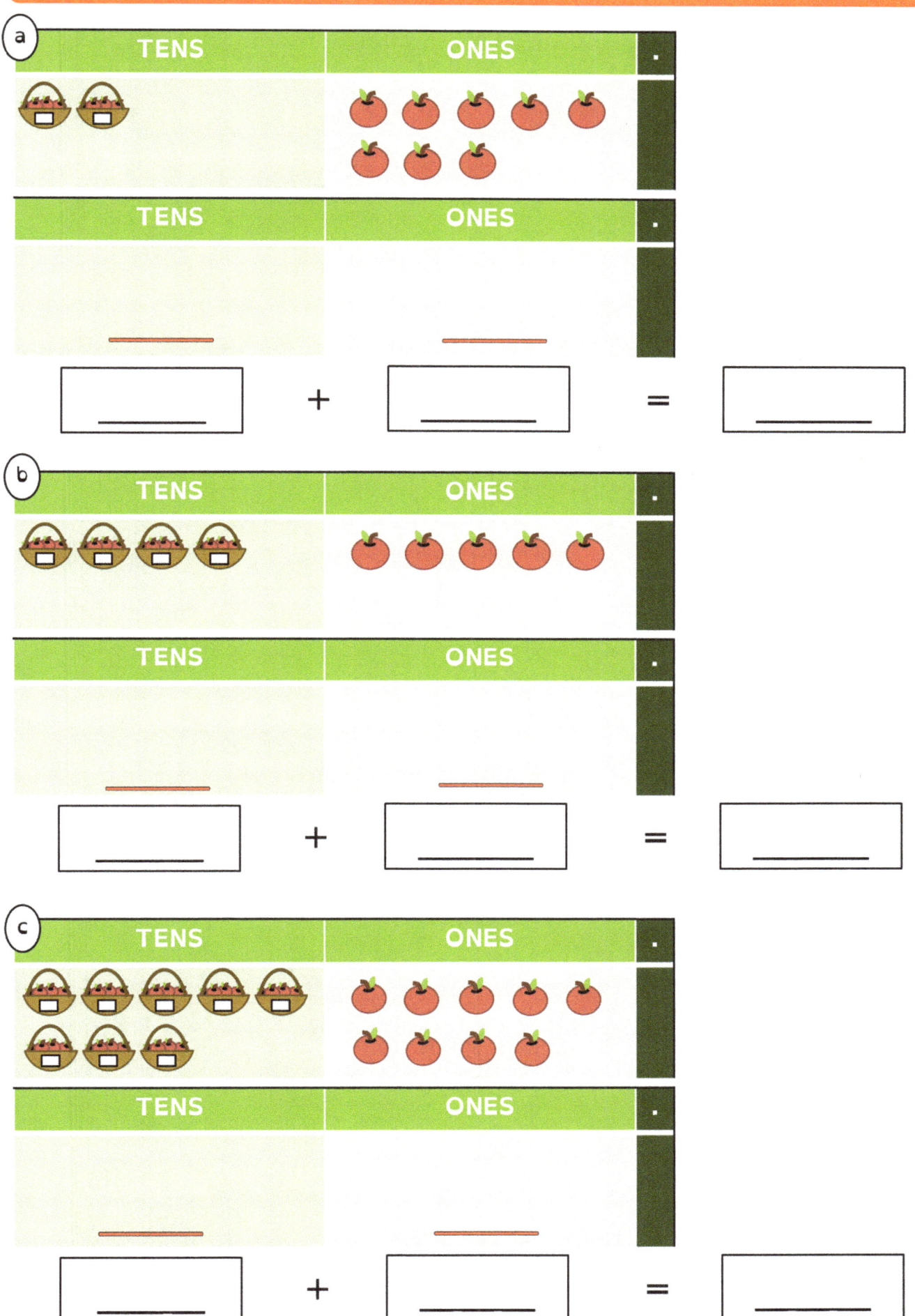

4. Fill in the gaps and complete each box like in the example below.

5. It's important to know how to split something into the tens and ones from just looking at the number as well. It'll help heaps for when you're doing addition. So, let's work on that. Fill in the gaps.

e.g.

68

68

TENS	ONES	.
6	8	

___6___ tens
+ ___8___ ones
= 68

___60___ + ___8___

a)

29

29

TENS	ONES	.

_____ tens
+ _____ ones
= 29

_____ + _____

b)

73

73

TENS	ONES	.

_____ tens
+ _____ ones
= 73

_____ + _____

6. A few more exercises ...
You will know you've got it when it feels too easy!

a)

54

54

____ tens
+ ____ ones
= 54

TENS	ONES	.

[____] + [____]

b)

86

86

____ tens
+ ____ ones
= 86

TENS	ONES	.

[____] + [____]

c)

31

31

____ tens
+ ____ ones
= 31

TENS	ONES	.

[____] + [____]

7. Fill in the missing numbers here too.

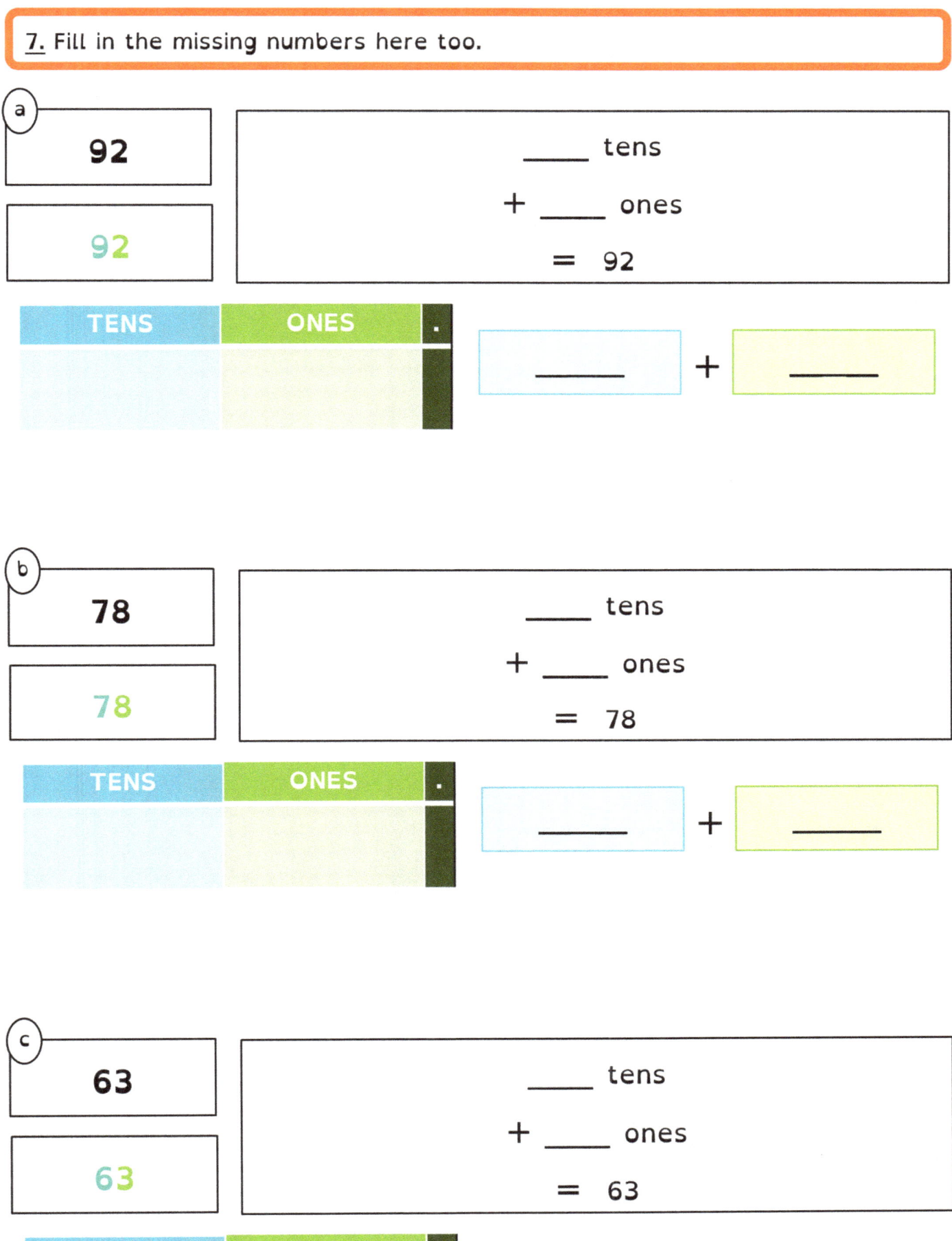

ANSWERS: The number line & tidy numbers

Page 25

<u>1.</u>
a. 5 in the tens column, final number: 50
b. 9 in the tens column, final number: 90
c. 6 in the tens column, final number 60

Page 26

<u>2.</u>
a. 3 in the tens column, 30 + 0 = 30
b. 6 in the tens column, 60 + 0 = 60

Page 27

<u>3.</u>
a. 2 in the tens column, 8 in the ones column, final number: 28. 20 + 8 = 28
b. 4 in the tens column, 5 in the ones column, final number: 45. 40 + 5 = 45
c. 8 in the tens column, 9 in the ones column, final number: 89. 80 + 9 = 89

Page 28

<u>4.</u>
a. 80 + 6 = 8 tens + 6 ones = 86
b. 20 + 4 = 2 tens + 4 ones = 24
c. 50 + 3 = 5 tens + 3 ones = 53

ANSWERS: The number line & tidy numbers

Page 29

5.
a. 29 = 2 tens + 9 ones = 20 + 9
b. 73 = 7 tens + 3 ones = 70 + 3

Page 30

6.
a. 54 = 5 tens + 4 ones = 50 + 4
b. 86 = 8 tens + 6 ones = 80 + 6
c. 31 = 3 tens + 1 one = 30 + 1

Page 31

7.
a. 92 = 9 tens + 2 ones = 90 + 2
b. 78 = 7 tens + 8 ones = 70 + 8
c. 63 = 6 tens + 3 ones = 60 + 3

Into the hundreds and thousands

What happens when we get even more apples? Bigger numbers! Into the hundreds, to be exact.

Say hello to the hundreds column – it works the same as the other columns.

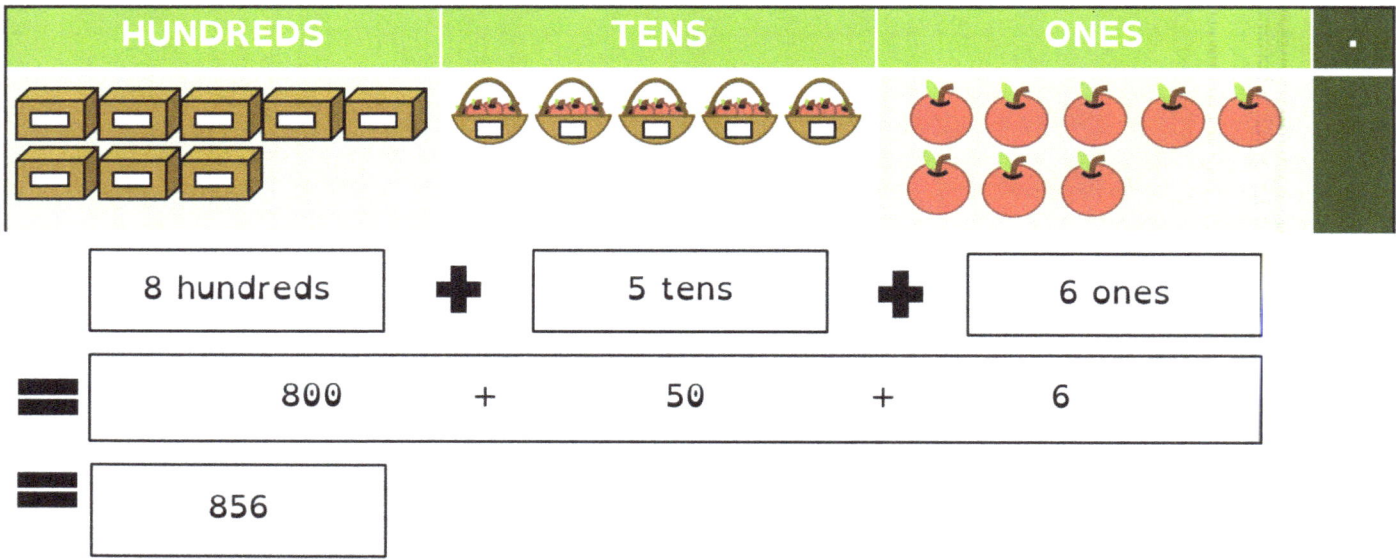

HUNDREDS	TENS	ONES

8 hundreds + 5 tens + 6 ones
= 800 + 50 + 6
= 856

Look below. See how the 0 acts as a placeholder when there's nothing in the tens column?

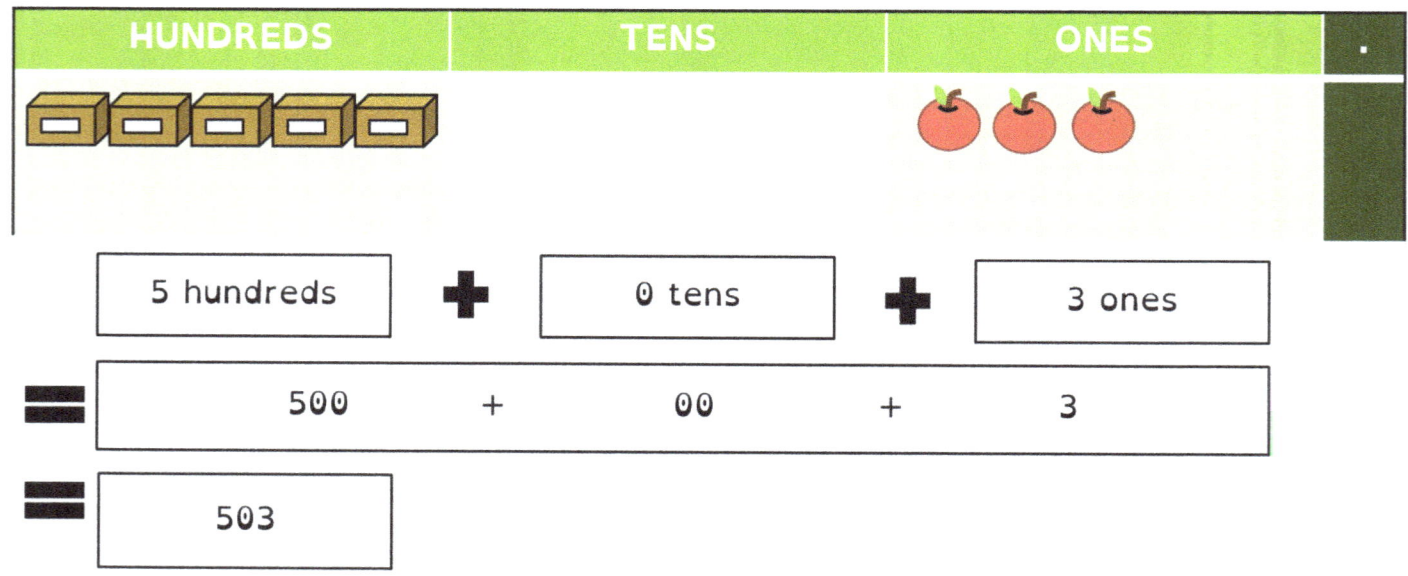

5 hundreds + 0 tens + 3 ones
= 500 + 00 + 3
= 503

Zero (0) also help us know how to add the numbers up properly. Every number has a sneaky invisible decimal point after the ones column, but usually mathematicians only write the decimal point if the number has decimals in it.

Decimals represent parts of a whole, which we'll learn about later. For now, just know that the decimal point comes right after the ones column.

Note: it doesn't matter how many zeros we add after the decimal point for any number, as the value doesn't change. Here are some examples:

800 = 800.0

50 = 50.0

6 = 6.0

800	800.0	800.00000	800.
50	50.0000	50.00	50.000
6	6.0	6.0000000	6.00

When you're adding numbers, make sure you line them up so each number's place values are in the same column. You want the ones above ones, tens above tens, etc. The easiest way is to do that with the decimal point.

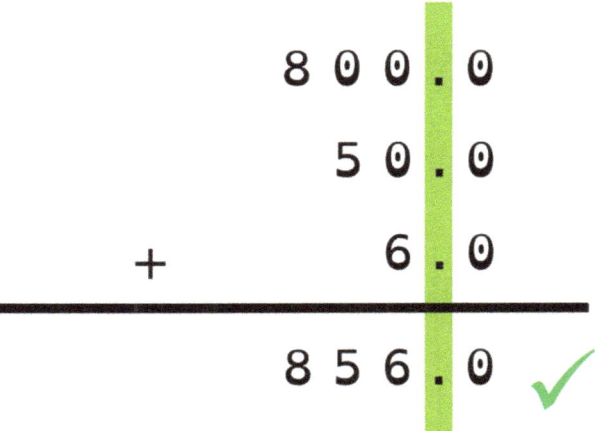

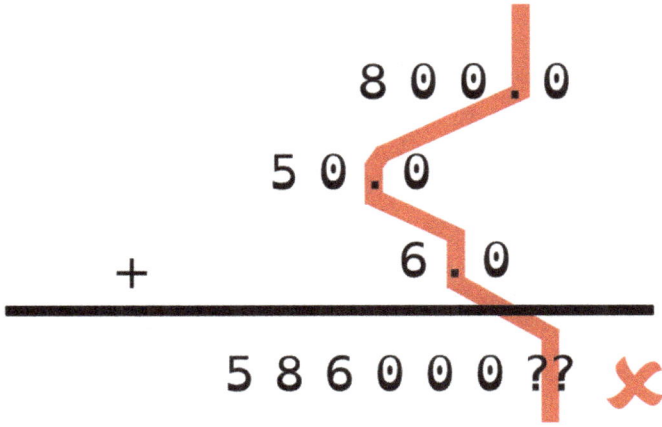

If we don't line up our place values properly, things could become very strange indeed ...

If you can see how to line the numbers up in your head, that's great. If you can't yet, a grid can be helpful, like the one here:

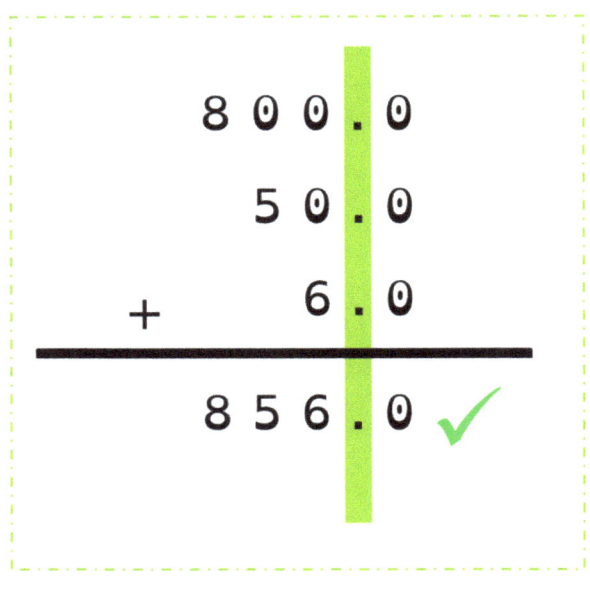

Different ways to line up
800 + 50 + 6 = 856

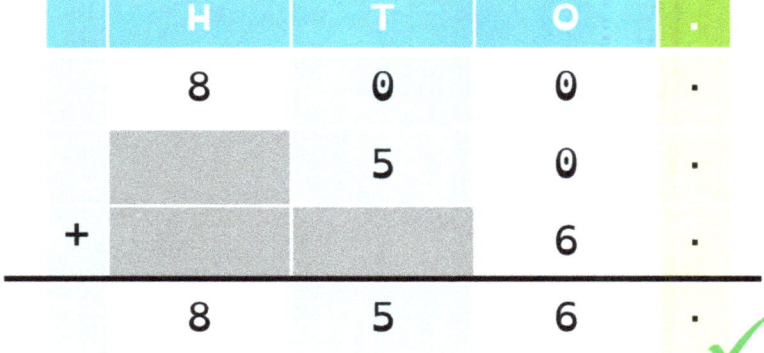

1. Now have a go yourself. Give it a try without using the blue chart first, but if you find you need it, it's there for you.

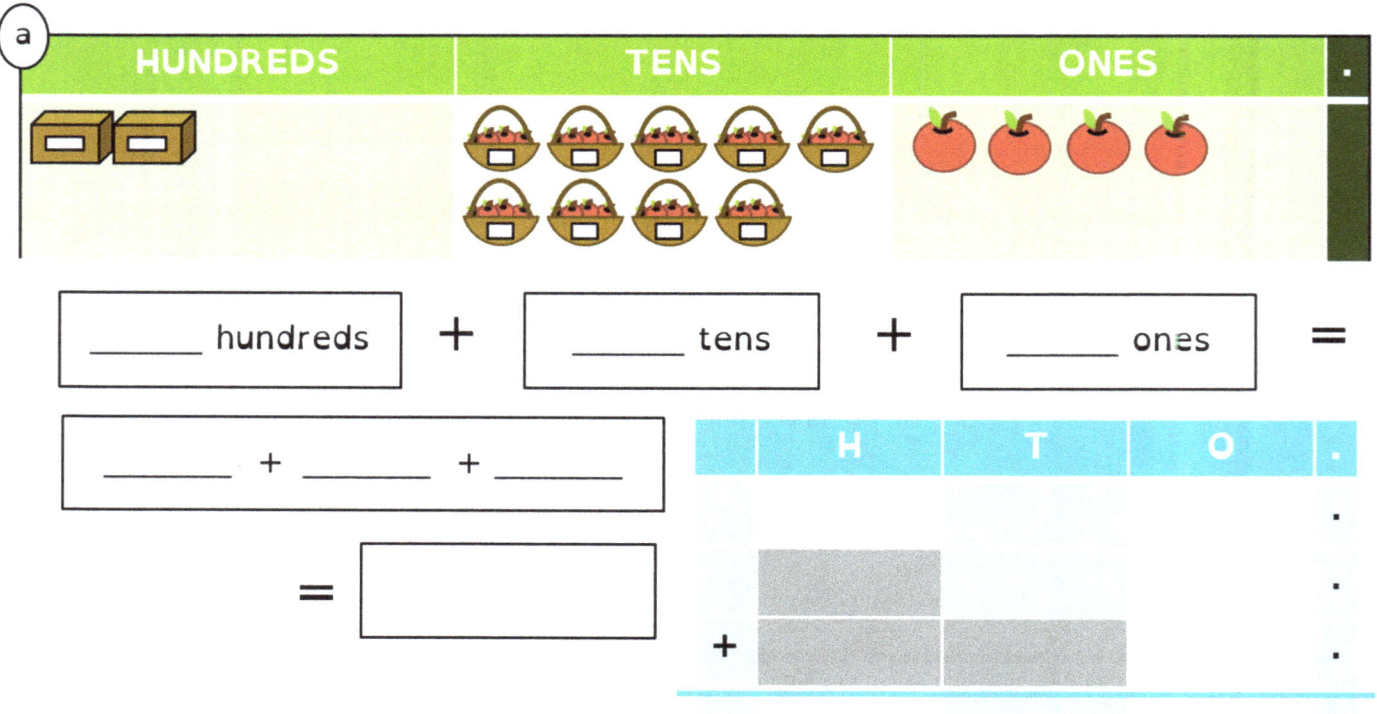

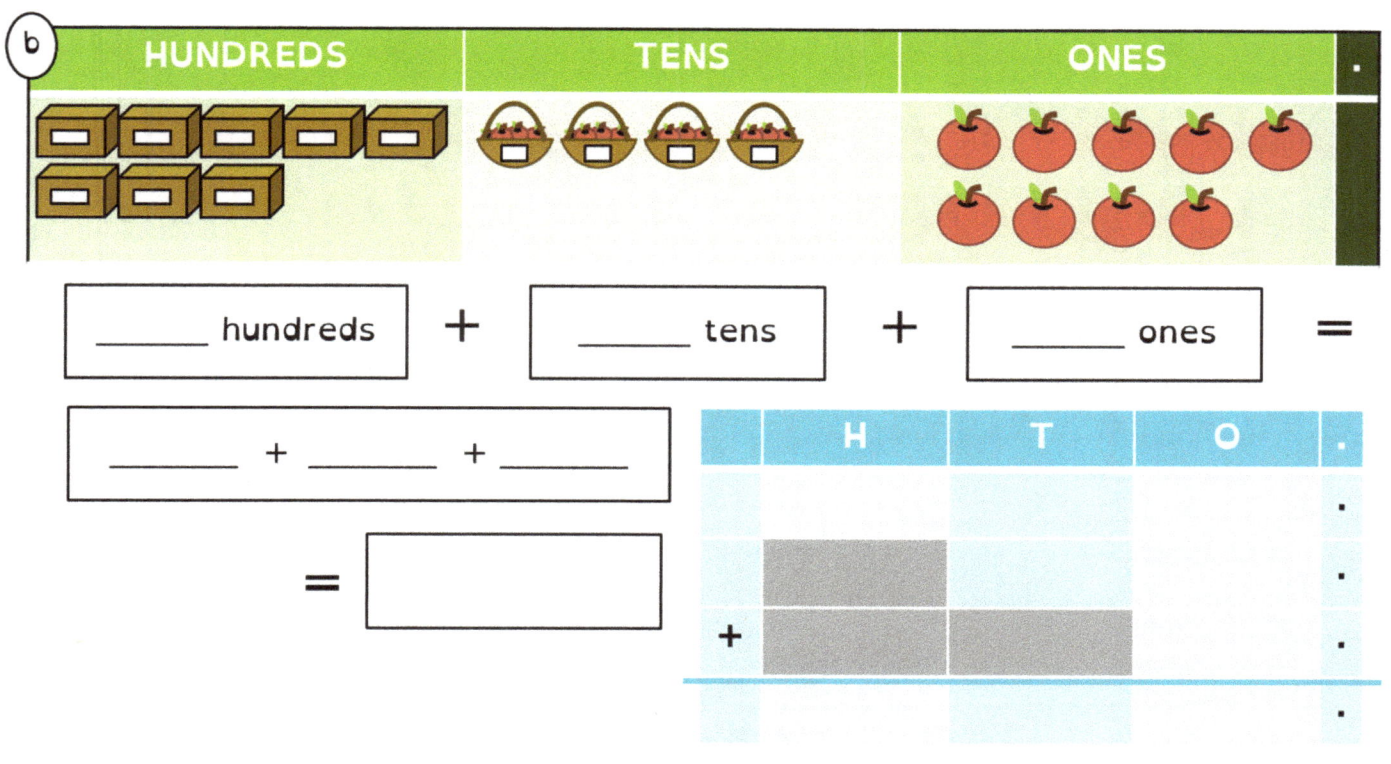
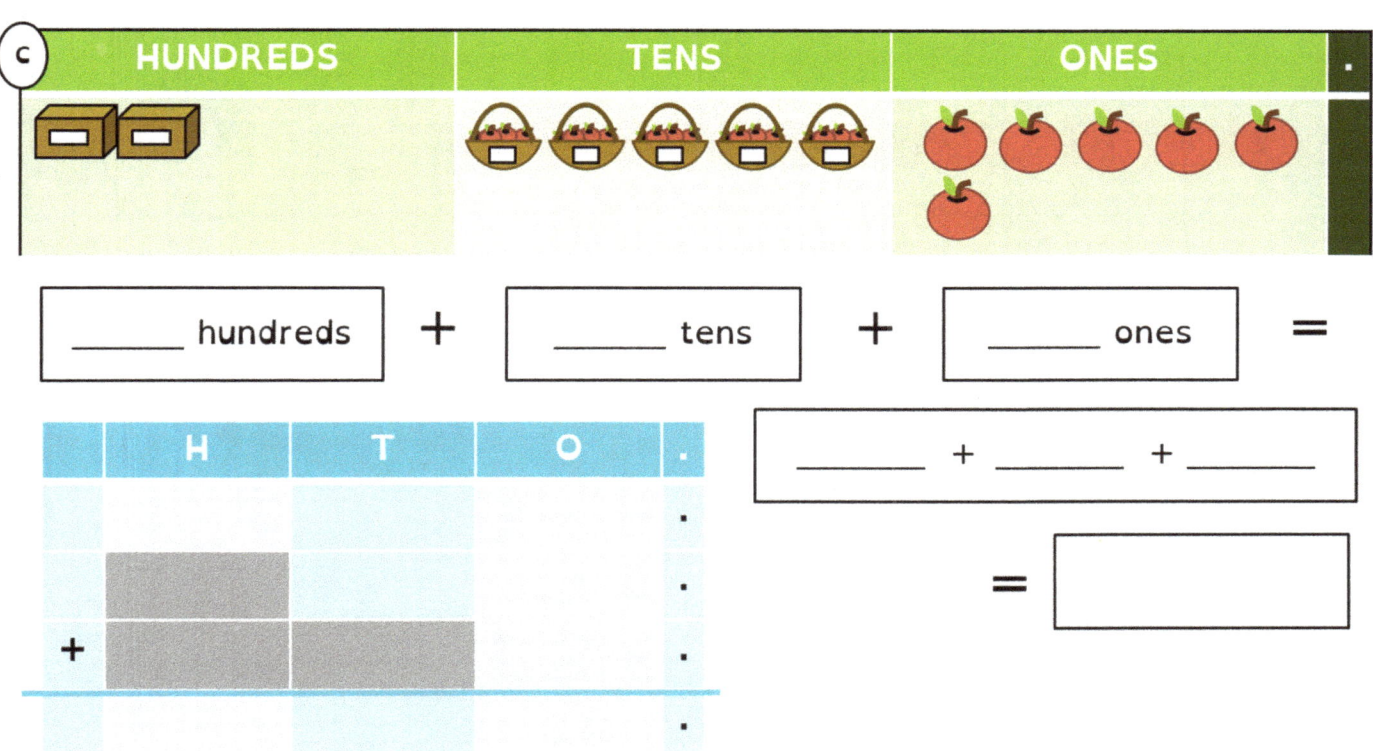
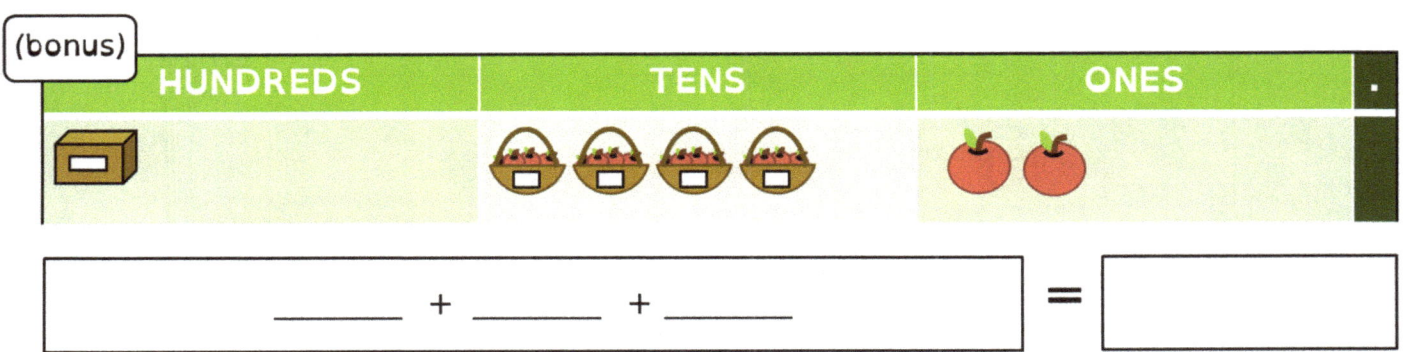

d

HUNDREDS	TENS	ONES
4 boxes	6 baskets	8 apples

____ hundreds + ____ tens + ____ ones

= ____ + ____ + ____   = ____

e

HUNDREDS	TENS	ONES
1 box	8 baskets	2 apples

____ hundred + ____ tens + ____ ones

= ____ + ____ + ____   = ____

f

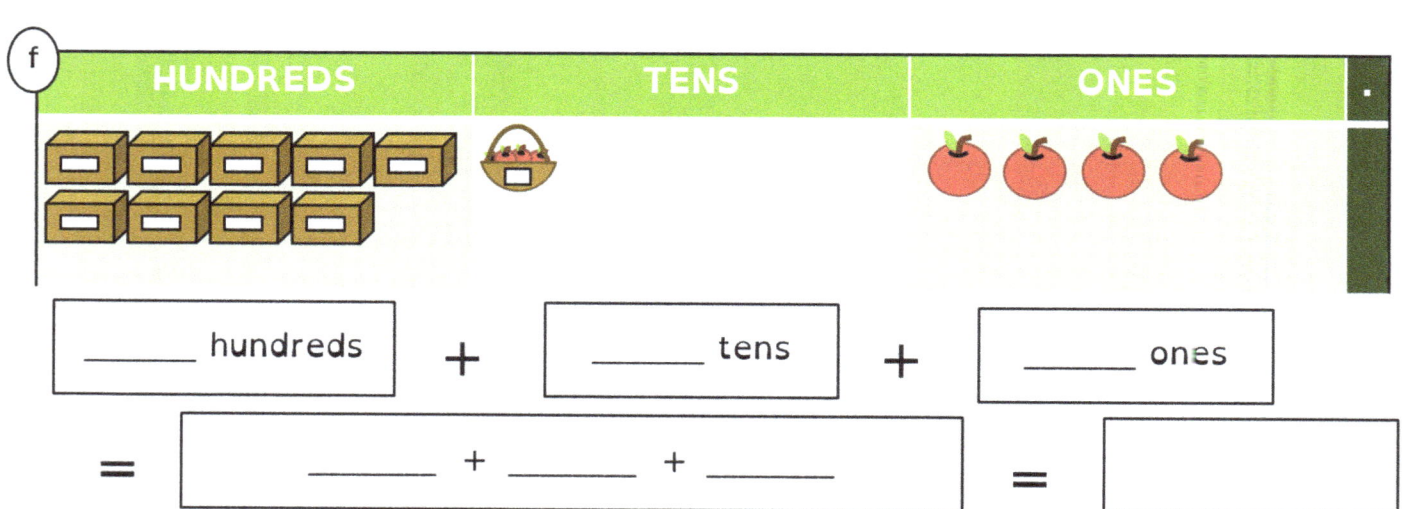

HUNDREDS	TENS	ONES
8 boxes	1 basket	4 apples

____ hundreds + ____ tens + ____ ones

= ____ + ____ + ____   = ____

g

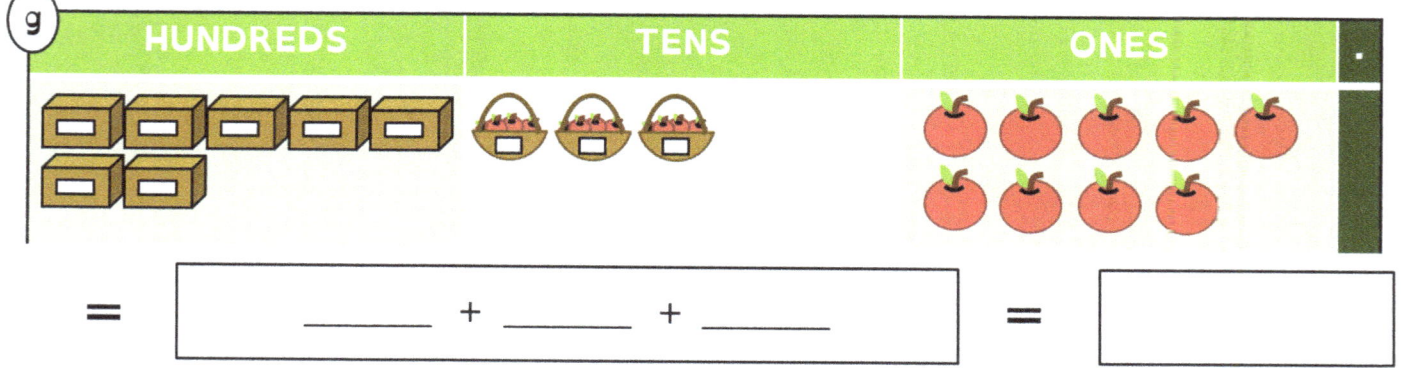

HUNDREDS	TENS	ONES
7 boxes	3 baskets	9 apples

= ____ + ____ + ____   = ____

2. Now we're going to split these back into their place values.

e.g. 184

184

__1__ hundred + __8__ tens + __4__ ones = 184

HUNDREDS	TENS	ONES	.
1	8	4	

__1__00 + __8__0 + __4__

a) 956

956

____ hundreds + ____ tens + ____ ones = 956

HUNDREDS	TENS	ONES	.

__00 + __0 + ____

b) 837

837

____ hundreds + ____ tens + ____ ones = 837

HUNDREDS	TENS	ONES	.

____ + ____ + ____

3. Here's another page for you:

a) 274

274

____ hundreds + ____ tens + ____ ones = 274

HUNDREDS	TENS	ONES	.

_____ + _____ + _____

b) 693

693

____ hundreds + ____ tens + ____ ones = 693

HUNDREDS	TENS	ONES	.

_____ + _____ + _____

c) 109

109

____ hundred + ____ tens + ____ ones = 109

HUNDREDS	TENS	ONES	.

_____ + _____ + _____

Guess what? There are still more apples! We're going to have to start packing boxes into trucks. Each truck fits 10 boxes, which means each truck will have a thousand apples.

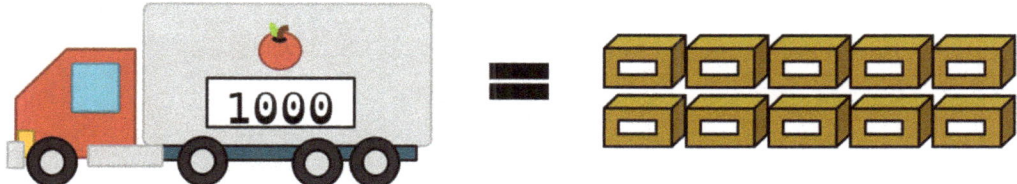

4. Fill in the equations below.

e.g.

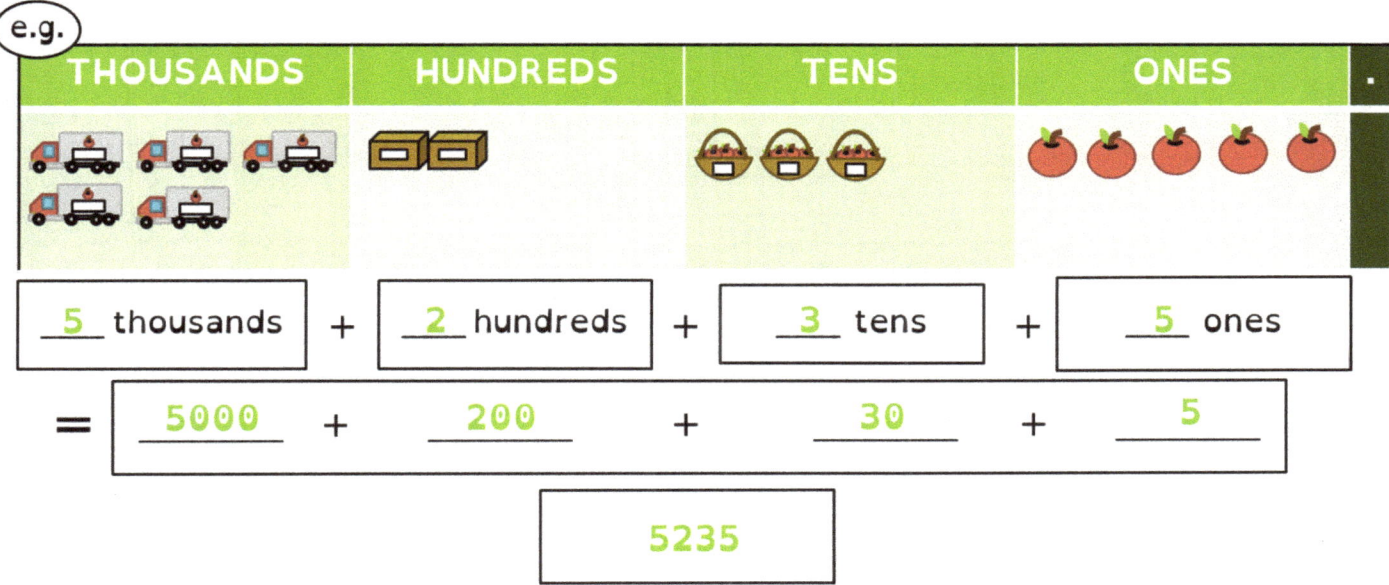

__5__ thousands + __2__ hundreds + __3__ tens + __5__ ones

= __5000__ + __200__ + __30__ + __5__

5235

a.

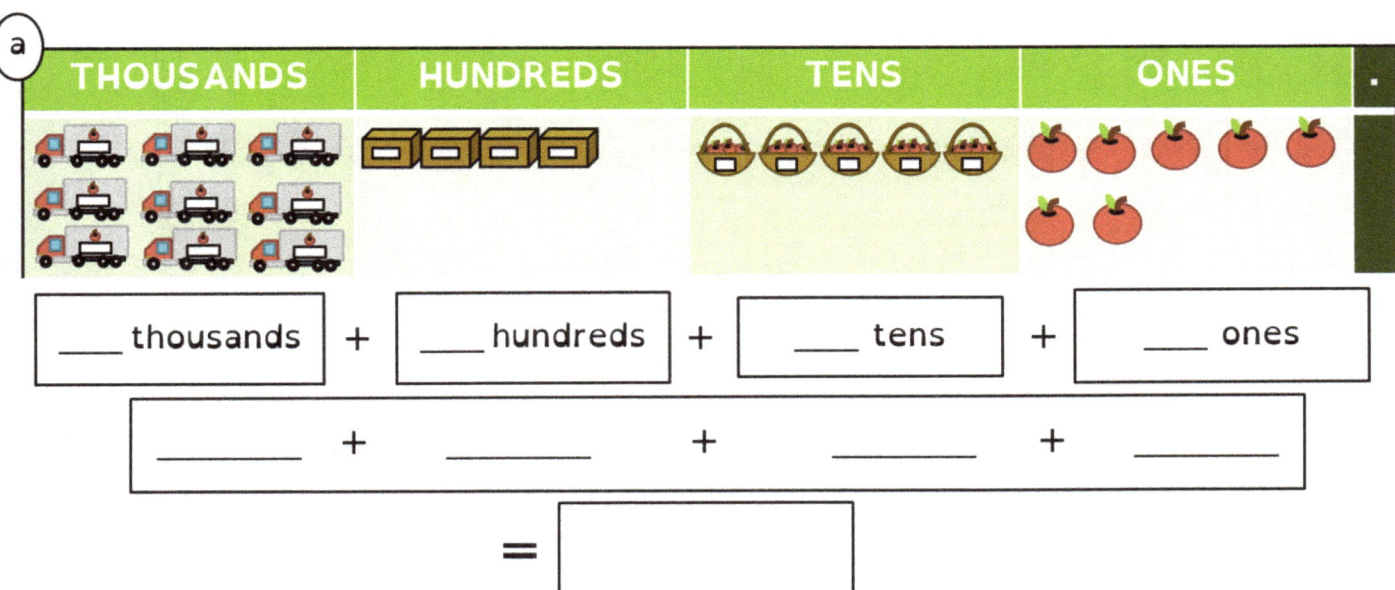

___ thousands + ___ hundreds + ___ tens + ___ ones

___ + ___ + ___ + ___

= ___

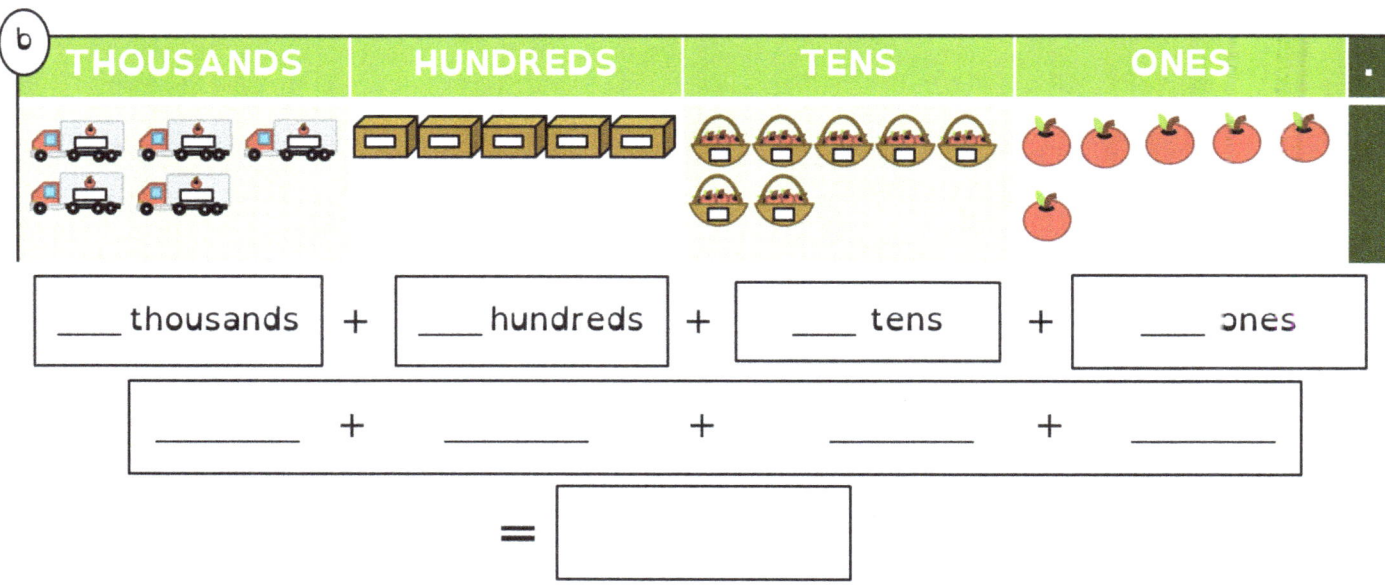

___ thousands + ___ hundreds + ___ tens + ___ ones

_____ + _____ + _____ + _____

= _____

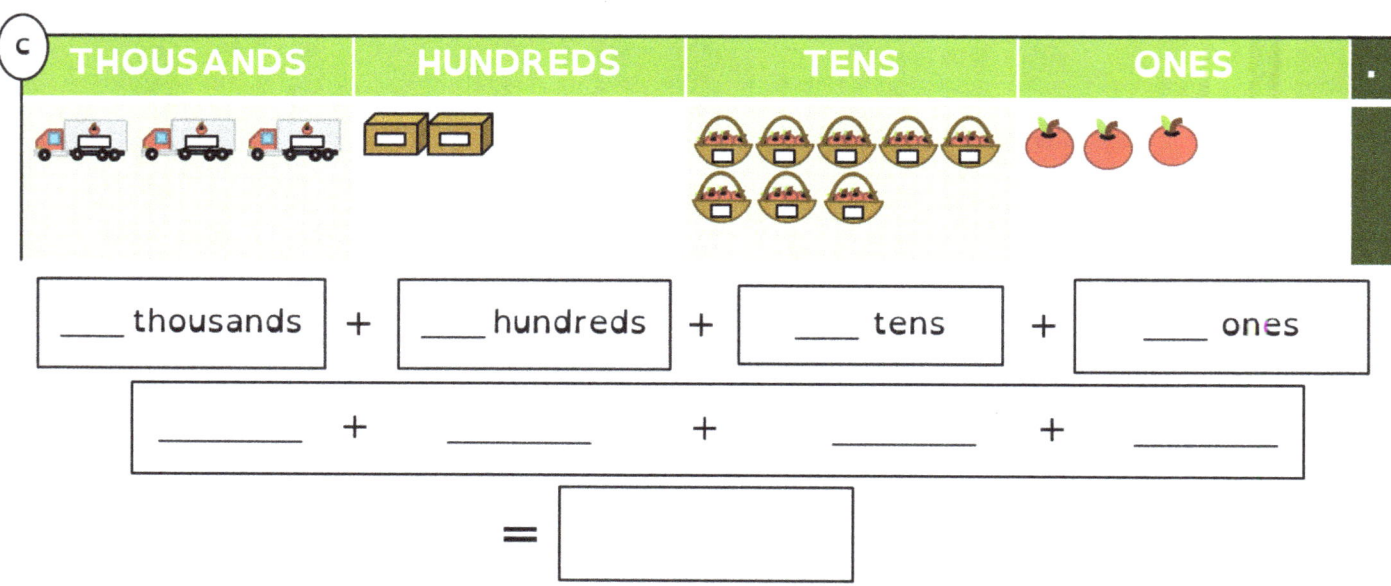

___ thousands + ___ hundreds + ___ tens + ___ ones

_____ + _____ + _____ + _____

= _____

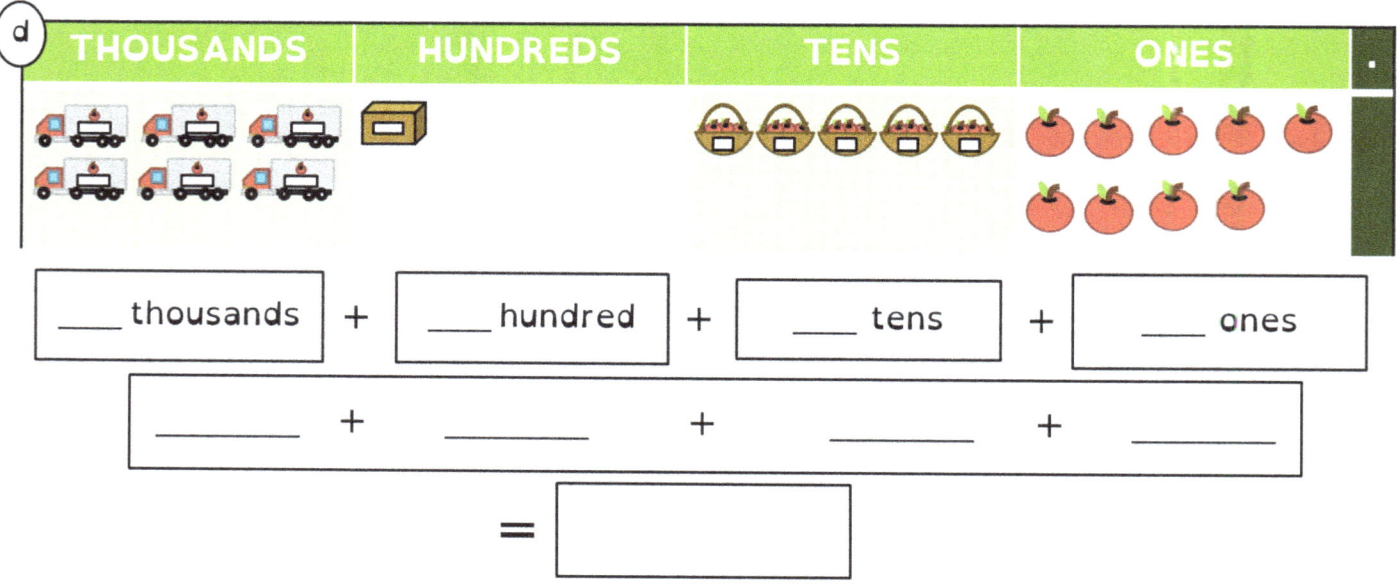

___ thousands + ___ hundred + ___ tens + ___ ones

_____ + _____ + _____ + _____

= _____

e)

THOUSANDS	HUNDREDS	TENS	ONES
9 trucks	2 boxes	5 baskets	8 apples

___ thousands + ___ hundreds + ___ tens + ___ ones

_____ + _____ + _____ + _____

= _____

f)

THOUSANDS	HUNDREDS	TENS	ONES
5 trucks	2 boxes	7 baskets	4 apples

___ thousands + ___ hundreds + ___ tens + ___ ones

_____ + _____ + _____ + _____

= _____

g)

THOUSANDS	HUNDREDS	TENS	ONES
7 trucks	3 boxes	5 baskets	5 apples

___ thousands + ___ hundreds + ___ tens + ___ ones

_____ + _____ + _____ + _____

= _____

43

ANSWERS: Into the hundreds and thousands

Page 36

<u>1.</u>

a. 2 hundreds + 9 tens + 4 ones = 200 + 90 + 4 = 294

Page 37

b. 8 hundreds + 4 tens + 9 ones = 800 + 40 + 9 = 849
c. 2 hundreds + 5 tens + 6 ones = 200 + 50 + 6 = 256
(bonus) 100 + 40 + 2 = 142

Page 38

d. 4 hundreds + 6 tens + 8 ones = 400 + 60 + 8 = 468
e. 1 hundred + 8 tens + 2 ones = 100 + 80 + 2 = 182
f. 9 hundreds + 9 tens + 4 ones = 900 + 90 + 4 = 994
g. 7 hundreds + 3 tens + 9 ones = 700 + 30 + 9 = 739

Page 39

<u>2.</u>

a. 956 = 2 hundreds + 5 tens + 6 ones = 200 + 50 + 6
b. 837 = 8 hundreds + 3 tens + 7 ones = 800 + 30 + 7

Page 40

<u>3.</u>

a. 274 = 2 hundreds + 7 tens + 4 ones = 200 + 70 + 4
b. 693 = 6 hundreds + 9 tens + 3 ones = 600 + 90 + 3
c. 109 = 1 hundred + 0 tens + 9 ones = 100 + 0 + 9

ANSWERS: Into the hundreds and thousands

Page 41

<u>4.</u>

a. 9 thousands + 4 hundreds + 5 tens + 7 ones
   = 9000 + 400 + 50 + 7 = 9457

Page 42

b. 5 thousands + 5 hundreds + 7 tens + 6 ones
   = 5000 + 500 + 70 + 6 = 5576
c. 3 thousands + 2 hundreds + 8 tens + 3 ones
   = 3000 + 200 + 80 + 3 = 3283
d. 6 thousands + 1 hundred + 5 tens + 9 ones
   6000 + 100 + 50 + 9 = 6159

Page 43

e. 9 thousands + 2 hundreds + 5 tens + 8 ones
   = 9000 + 200 + 50 + 8 = 9258
f. 4 thousands + 2 hundreds + 9 tens + 4 ones
   4000 + 200 + 90 + 4 = 4294
g. 7 thousands + 3 hundreds + 6 tens + 5 ones
   7000 + 300 + 60 + 5 = 7365

Counting and word problems

Now it's time to take a super close look at adding. When we're adding small numbers, it's easiest just to count.

Remember what each digit represents:

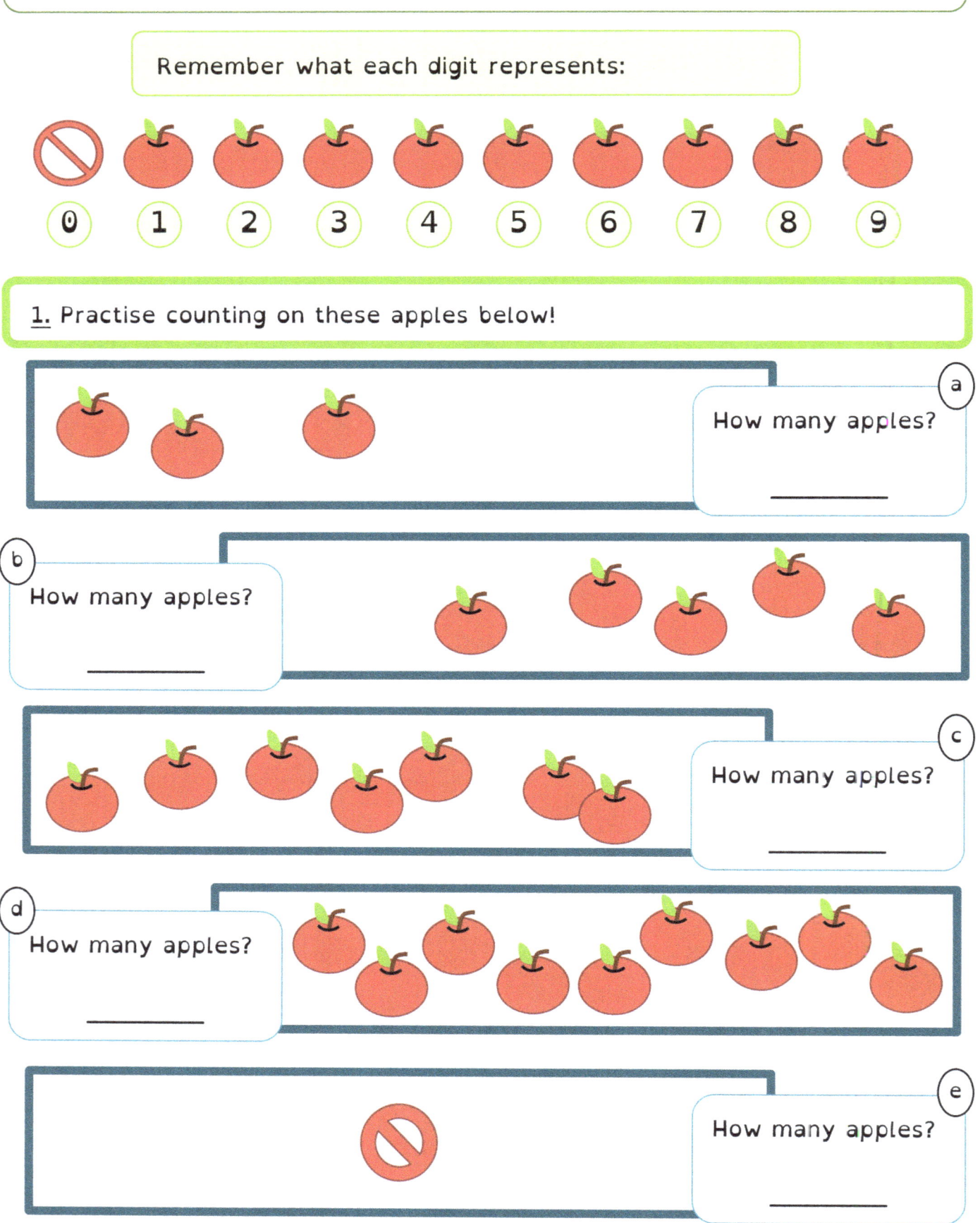

1. Practise counting on these apples below!

a. How many apples? _____

b. How many apples? _____

c. How many apples? _____

d. How many apples? _____

e. How many apples? _____

Adding is just like counting multiple groups of apples, one after the other!

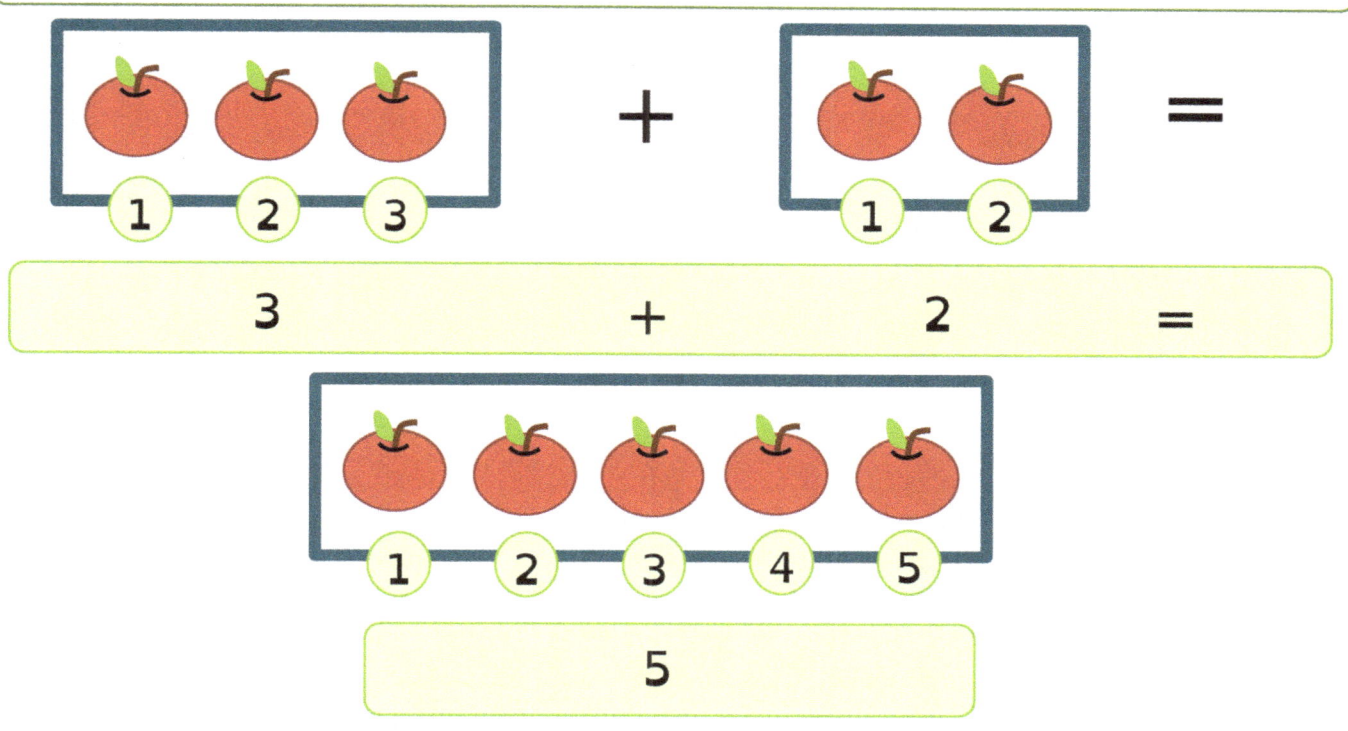

Here's what that equation could look like as a word problem:

Barry has three apples, then picks two more. How many apples does he now have in total?

Doris eats three apples on Monday, and then two apples on Tuesday. How many apples did she eat in total?

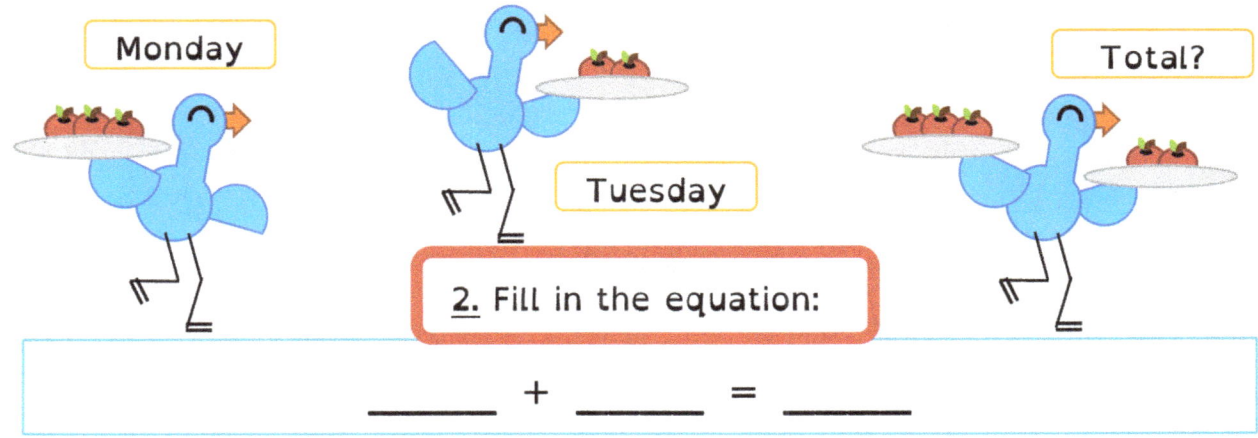

2. Fill in the equation:

____ + ____ = ____

3. Solve these questions, then fill in the missing words to complete the word equation.

a) 2 + 7 = _____

Doris eats _____ apples, then eats _____ more.

How many apples has she eaten in total?

b) 4 + 3 = _____

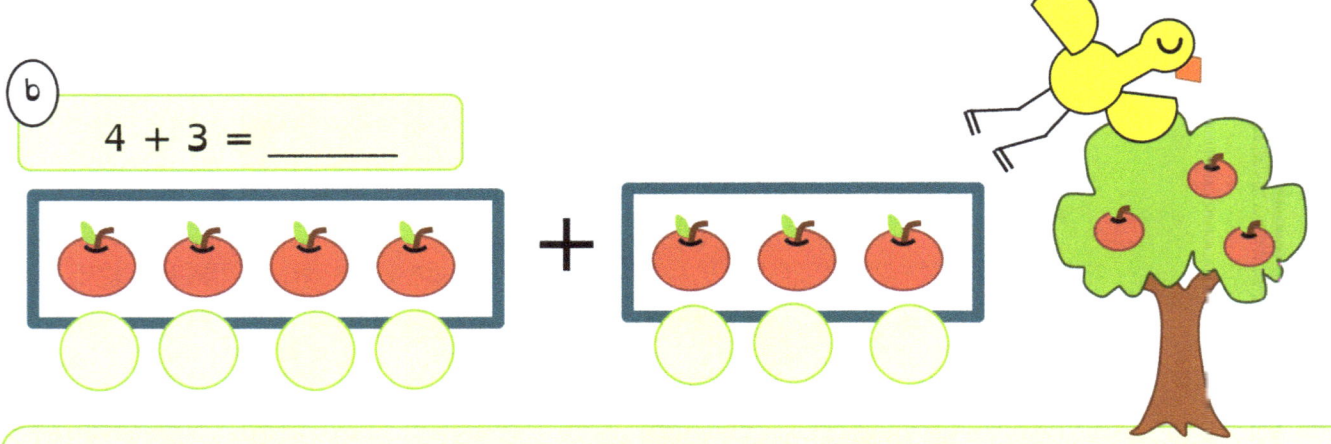

Barry has _____ apples, then picks _____ more.

How many apples does he have now?

c) 5 + 1 = _____

Doris buys _____ apples, then buys _____ more.

How many apples did she buy in total?

d) 1 + 2 + 1 = _____

Barry eats _____ apple, bakes a cake using _____ apples, then puts _____ apple into his lunchbox for tomorrow.
How many apples did he use in total?

e) 3 + 1 + 2 = _____

Doris makes apple juice from _____ apples, snacks on _____ apple, then bakes a pie using _____ apples. How many apples did she use altogether?

f) 5 + 3 + 1 = _____

Barry makes apple jam using _____ apples, fruit salad using _____ apples, and then eats _____ more.
How many apples did he use in total?

4. Have a go at these mixed problems.

a) 3 + 5 = _____

b) Doris has two apples, then picks four more. How many apples does she have now?

____ + ____ = ____

c) 4 + 1 = ____

____ + ____ = ____

d) Barry has three apples, then picks six more. How many apples does he have now?

____ + ____ = ____

ANSWERS: Counting and word problems

Page 46

<u>1.</u>

a. 3   b. 5   c. 7   d. 9   e. 0

Page 47

<u>2.</u> 3 + 2 = 5

Page 48

<u>3.</u>

a. Doris eats 2 apples, then eats 7 more. She has eaten 9 apples in total. 2 + 7 = 9
b. Barry has 4 apples, then picks 3 more. He now has 7 apples. 4 + 3 = 7
c. Doris buys 5 apples, then buys 1 more. She has bought 6 apples in total. 5 + 1 = 6

Page 49

d. Barry eats 1 apple, bakes a cake using 2 apples, then puts 1 apple into his lunchbox for tomorrow. He used 4 apples in total. 1 + 2 + 1 = 4
e. Doris makes apple juice from 3 apples, snacks on 1 apple, then bakes a pie using 2 apples. She used 6 apples altogether. 3 + 1 + 2 = 6
f. Barry makes apple jam using 5 apples, fruit salad using 3 apples, and then eats 1 more. He used 9 apples in total. 5 + 3 + 1 = 9.

Page 50

<u>4.</u>

a. 8   b. 2 + 4 = 6   c. 5   d. 3 + 6 = 9

Algebra

We can write addition equations in formats other than just numbers. This is algebra. Algebra is where we use symbols other than numbers to represent a 'mystery number' that we don't know yet!

apple + apple = _____ apples

1 apple + 1 apple = 2 apples

Instead of using words or numbers to represent things, we can also use letters. Let's say we use the letter 'a' instead of the word 'apple' above.

[apple] + [apple] = 2 [apples]

$a + a = 2a$

Note: 'a' can also be written as '1a'

1. Give algebra a go!

a) $2a + 3a = $ _____

a (or 1a), 2a | a (or 1a), 2a, 3a | a (or 1a), 2a, 3a, 4a, 5a

b) $3a + 1a = $ _____

52

c) 2 + 4 = ____

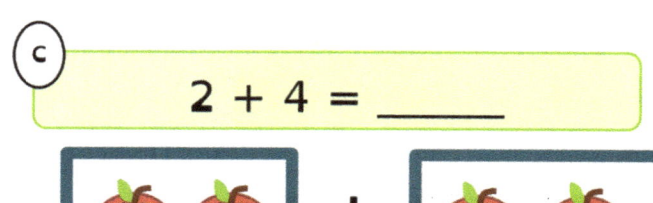

d) 2a + 4a = ____

e) 6 + 1 = ____

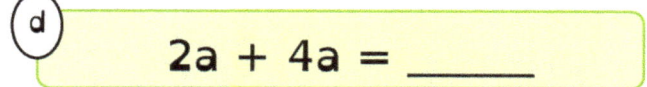

f) 6a + (1)a = ____

g) 3a + a + 2a = ____

You might have seen algebraic equations with a bunch of different letters in them. Since those letters are all just representing their own 'mystery number', we can think of them as we do with different fruits. For example, apples and pears are different fruits. This means we can add apples with apples and pears with pears, but we can't add apples together with pears.

p + p = 2p   a + a = 2a

Different types of fruit can't be added together, and different letters can't be added either. The equation just stays the same.

p + a = a + p

Usually we write the letters in alphabetical order, but it's not wrong if we don't.

Here's an example we can take a closer look at:

pear + pear + pear + apple = _____

Or
a + p + p + p
or
p + a + p + p
or
p + p + a + p

= p, 2p, 3p + a

The last two can also be written as:

a + 3p

= 3p + a

2. These questions use a range of different symbols to represent numbers, but the idea is always the same.

a) 💧 + ★ + ★ + ★ = _____

[💧] + [★ ★ ★] = [💧 + 3★]
(or 1💧)   (or 1★)   1★ 2★ 3★

b) 💧 + 💧 + ★ + ★ + ★ + ★ = _____

[💧 💧] + [★ ★ ★ ★] = [__💧 + __★]
 1💧 _2💧   1★ _2★ _3★ _4★

c) 3💧 + 3★ + 💧 = _____

[💧 💧 💧] + [★ ★ ★] + [💧] = [__💧 + __★]

d) ★ + 💧 + ★ + 💧 + ★ + 2💧 = _____

[★] + [💧] + [★] + [💧] + [★] + [💧 💧]

= [__💧 + __★]

e   a + b + b + b = _____

[a] + [b b b] = [a + __b]
 a   b 2b 3b
(or 1a)   (or 1b)

f   2a + 3b + a = _____

[a a] + [b b b] + [a] = [__a + __b]

g   x + x + x + y + y + y + y + y = _____

[x x x] + [y y y y y] = [__x + __y]

h   y + y + y + x + x + x + y + y = _____

[y y y] + [x x x] + [y y] = [___ + ___]

i   3y + 2x + 2y = _____

[y y y] + [x x] + [y y] = [___ + ___]

ANSWERS: Algebra

Page 52

1.
a. 5a
b. 4a

Page 53

c. 6
d. 6a
e. 7
f. 7a
g. 6

Page 54 – on next page

Page 56

2.
a. 1 ⬤ + 3 ★
b. 2 ⬤ + 4 ★
c. 4 ⬤ + 3 ★
d. 2 ⬤ + 3 ★

Page 57

e. a + 3b
f. 3a + 3b
g. 3x + 5y
h. 3x + 5y (or 5y + 3x)
i. 2x + 5y (or 5y + 2x)

Page 54: Example solution. You might have matched a different leaf and apple but the number is the same.

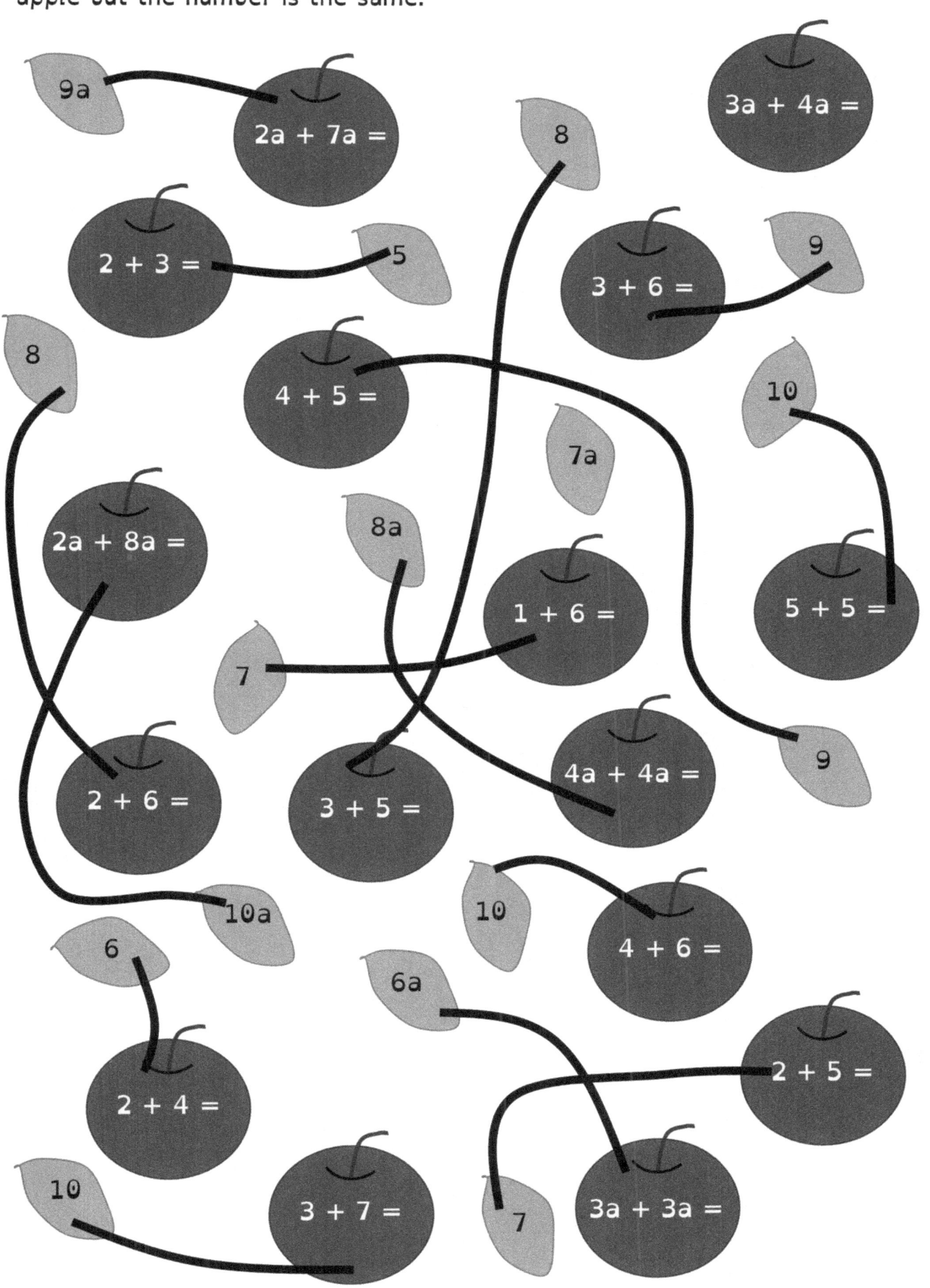

Behind the Scenes of Addition

Let's take a closer look at what happens on the number line when we're adding. What's actually happening when we calculate 1 + 1?
Why is it 2, and not 3 or 9 or 183745?

Adding is just starting on a number, and then moving towards the positive (+) side of the number line!

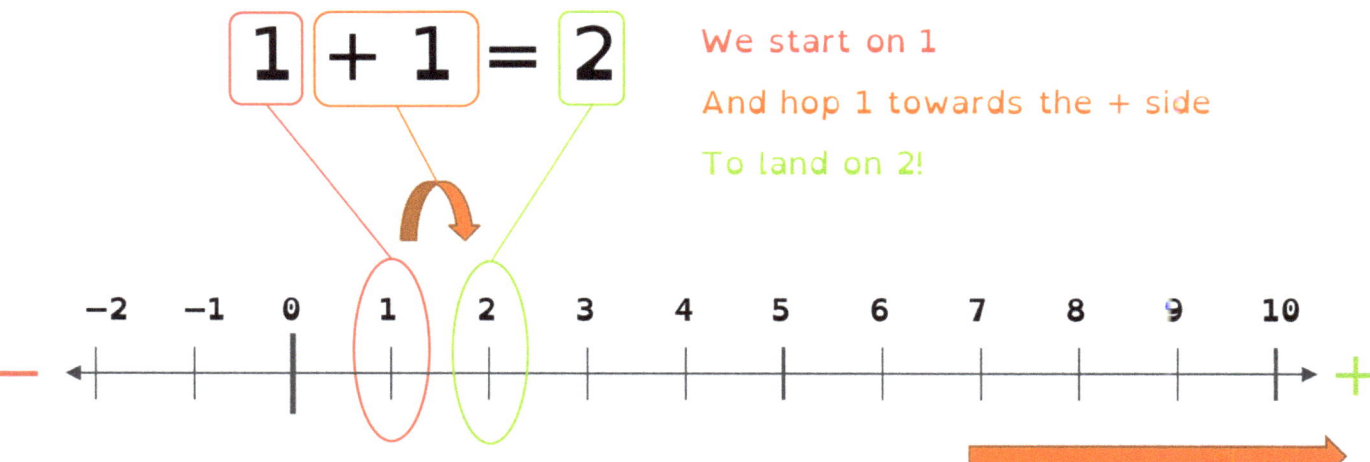

With shapes, it looks like this:

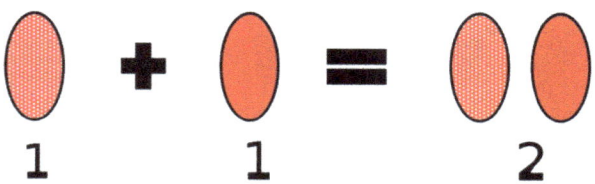

And on a snapshot of the hundred square, like this:

1	2	3	4
11	12	13	14

All addition equations can be represented in all these ways!

Let's use this equation to have a closer look at the nuts and bolts of addition. Here's an equation:

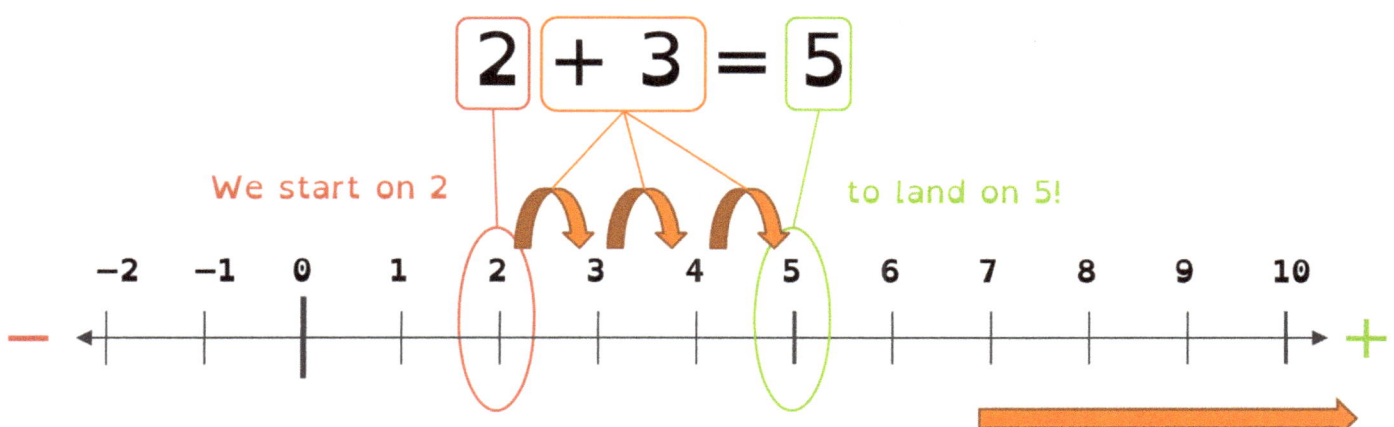

With shapes, it looks like this:

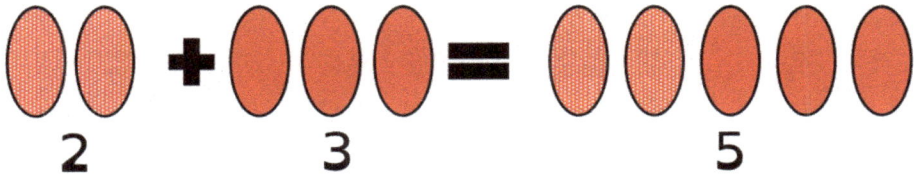

And on a snapshot of the hundred square, like this:

$2 + 3 = 5$

Now, if $2 + 3 = 5$, what do you think $3 + 2$ equals? And why?

If you said that 3 + 2 is also 5, that would be correct! If you know one addition equation, you actually know two! In any addition equation, you can swap the numbers you're adding together around, and the answer doesn't change.

Here's how the two equations look on the number line:

2 + 3 = 5

3 + 2 = 5

1. Let's get used to how we swap numbers around for addition.
Write the equation being shown on the number lines.

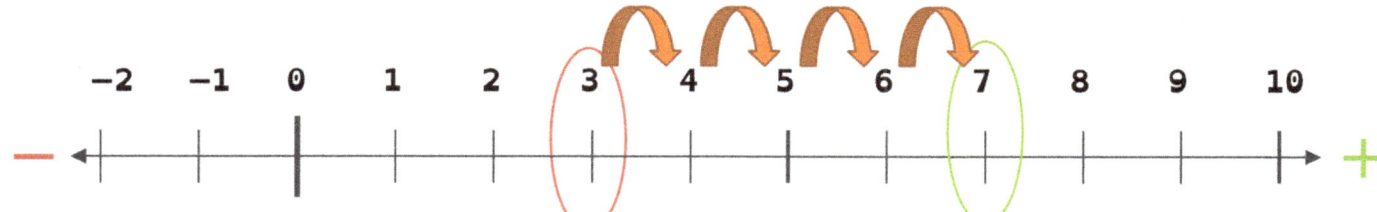

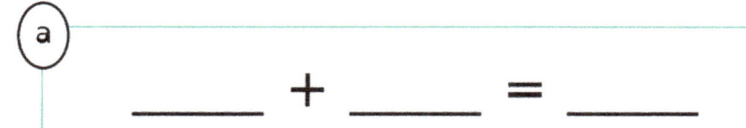
a) ____ + ____ = ____

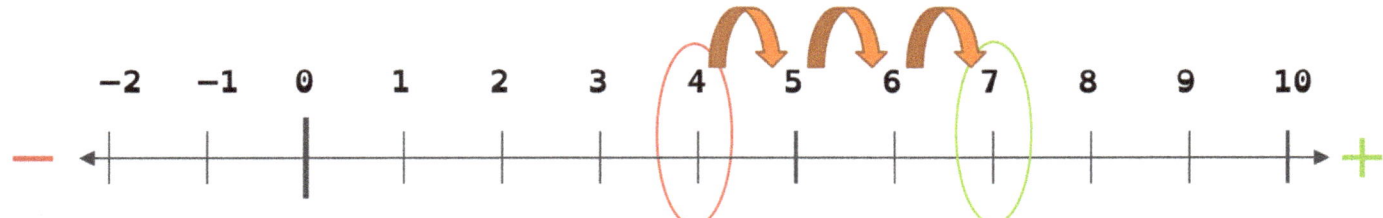

b) ____ + ____ = ____

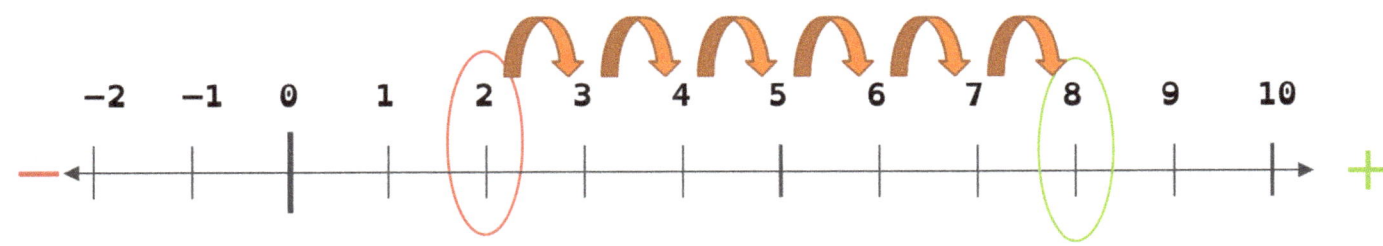

c) ____ + ____ = ____

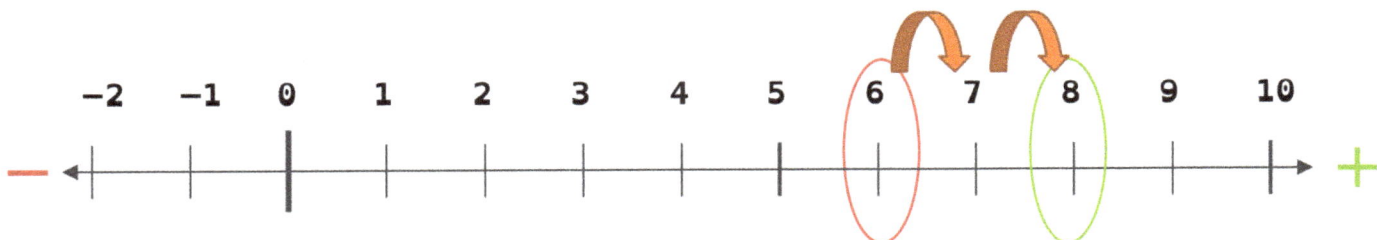

d) ____ + ____ = ____

2. Here's a few more, but this time it's your job to figure out the matching equation. Draw it on the blank number line too!

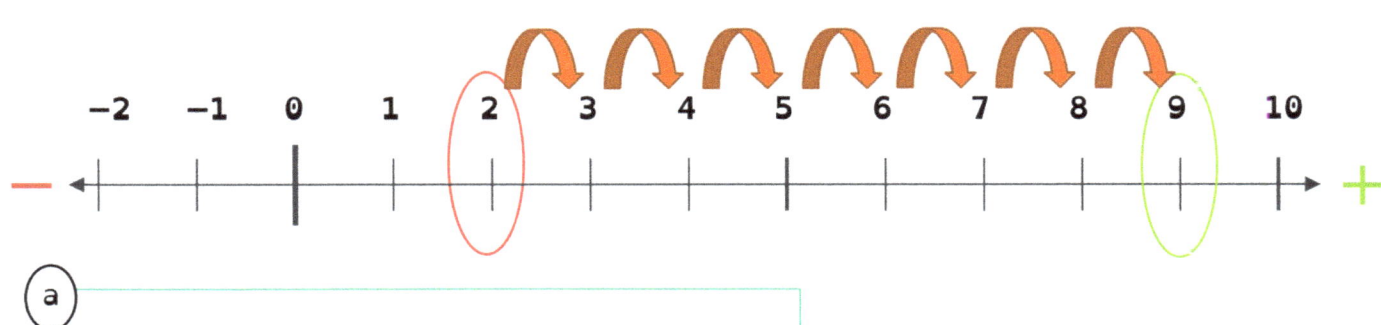

a) _____ + _____ = _____

b) _____ + _____ = _____

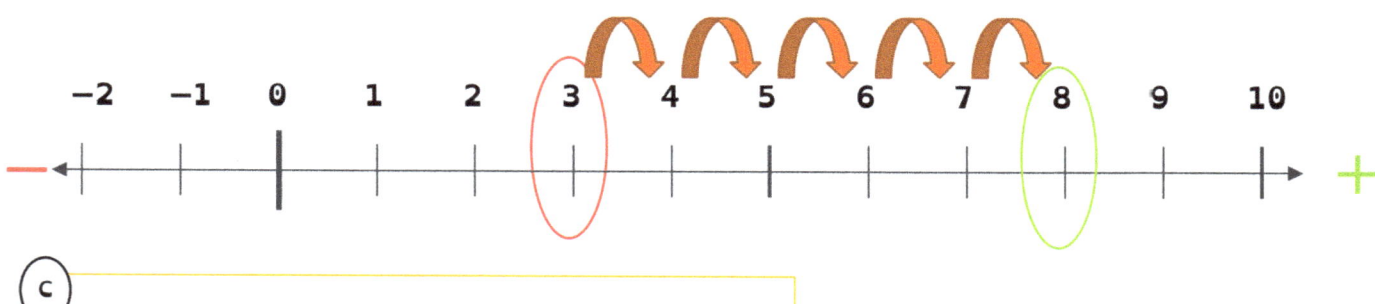

c) _____ + _____ = _____

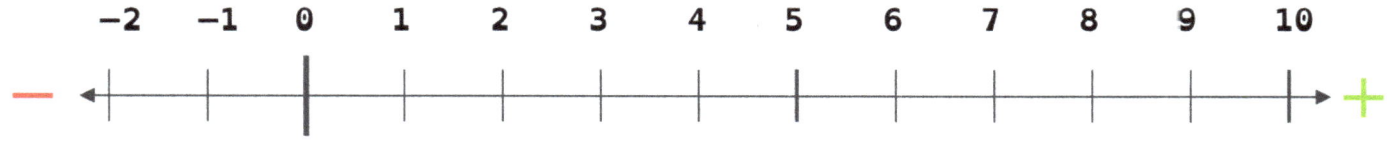

d) _____ + _____ = _____

3. Now let's do some questions without the number line.

e.g. If 2 + _3_ = 5   then   3 + _2_ = 5

a. If 7 + ___ = 9   then   2 + ___ = 9

b. If 5 + ___ = 9   then   4 + ___ = 9

c. If 1 + ___ = 4   then   3 + ___ = 4

d. If 6 + ___ = 8   then   2 + ___ = 8

4. This is the case with any addition equation you encounter. See if you can crack these questions.

a. If 16 + 3 = 19   then   3 + ___ = 19

b. If 22 + 8 = 30   then   8 + ___ = 30

c. If 47 + 11 = 58   then   11 + ___ = 58

d. If 65 + 32 = 97   then   32 + ___ = 97

e. If 104 + 58 = 162   then   58 + ___ = 162

ANSWERS: Behind the scenes of addition

Page 63

<u>1.</u>

a. 3 + 4 = 7
b. 4 + 3 = 7
c. 2 + 6 = 8
d. 6 + 2 = 8

Page 64

<u>2.</u>

a. 2 + 7 = 9
b. 7 + 2 = 9
c. 3 + 5 = 8
d. 5 + 3 = 8

Page 65

<u>3.</u>

a. If 7 + <u>2</u> = 9, then 2 + <u>7</u> = 9
b. If 5 + <u>4</u> = 9, then 4 + <u>5</u> = 9
c. If 1 + <u>3</u> = 4, then 3 + <u>1</u> = 4
d. If 6 + <u>2</u> = 8, then 2 + <u>6</u> = 8

<u>4.</u>

a. If 16 + 3 = 19, then 3 + <u>16</u> = 19
b. If 22 + 8 = 30, then 8 + <u>22</u> = 30
c. If 47 + 11 = 58, then 11 + <u>47</u> = 58
d. If 65 + 32 = 97, then 32 + <u>65</u> = 97
e. If 104 + 58 = 162, then 58 + <u>104</u> = 162

Mastering basic facts for zero to ten

For a smooth maths journey, we want to get to a place where we can say the answer to questions like 4 + 5 instantly, without thinking about it.

1. Using our fingers and counting is a good way to start. Let's warm up with these equations adding 1 first.

8 + 1 = _____   4 + 1 = _____

6 + 1 = _____   7 + 1 = _____

5 + 1 = _____   3 + 1 = _____

2 + 1 = _____   1 + 1 = _____

2. Now try these. We will do a set of these exact questions again later, so if you want to track your progress, ask someone to time you (and you can compare it with your time at the end).

4 + 4 = _____   3 + 6 = _____

3 + 2 = _____   5 + 3 = _____

3 + 3 = _____   4 + 2 = _____

4 + 5 = _____   2 + 5 = _____

6 + 2 = _____   4 + 3 = _____

6 + 3 = _____   2 + 2 = _____

Time:

Pictures can be a good way to help us remember our facts. We can help them stick in our head by making up some stories with them!

For example, for **2 + 3 = 5**

Snake attacked Swan, but Magician came to save her.

Here's one for **2 + 6 = 8**

When Swan blows the whistle, Honeybee flies over to play.

Here's one more story, and then it's your turn to make up your own! Draw or write your story, or do both. Unleash your imagination and creativity!

For example, for <u>3 + 4 = 7</u>

Because Snake tried to attack her friend Swan, Flamingo threw a Boomerang at Snake.

(Ask an adult for help if you need)

2 + 4 = 6 story:

5 + 2 = 7 story:

3 + 5 = 8 story:

2 + 2 = 4 story:

5 + 4 = 9 story:

2 + 7 = 9 story:

4 + 4 = 8 story:

3 + 6 = 9

3 + 6 = 9 story:

3 + 3 = 6

3 + 3 = 6 story:

Recall the story for each fact as you do it. Remember that the two adding numbers can be swapped around. For example, if you use the story for 2 + 3 to remember that it equals 5, then you also know the answer for 3 + 2. It's 5 as well.

If you prefer another strategy, like using your fingers or memory, that's fine! Use what works best for each equation.

3. Take your time with these!

(a)

3 + 2 = ____   8 + 0 = ____   7 + 2 = ____

8 + 1 = ____   3 + 5 = ____   3 + 2 = ____

2 + 4 = ____   3 + 1 = ____   5 + 0 = ____

7 + 2 = ____   6 + 3 = ____   2 + 5 = ____

(b)

2 + 7 = ____   1 + 2 = ____   2 + 6 = ____

4 + 5 = ____   2 + 3 = ____   6 + 1 = ____

2 + 6 = ____   3 + 4 = ____   5 + 4 = ____

4 + 3 = ____   1 + 7 = ____   3 + 3 = ____

(c)

3 + 4 = ____   2 + 7 = ____   6 + 1 = ____

9 + 0 = ____   3 + 4 = ____   2 + 4 = ____

7 + 1 = ____   4 + 5 = ____   5 + 2 = ____

2 + 2 = ____   4 + 4 = ____   2 + 3 = ____

(d)

3 + 5 = ___	2 + 7 = ___	6 + 1 = ___
8 + 1 = ___	3 + 4 = ___	2 + 2 = ___
7 + 1 = ___	1 + 5 = ___	5 + 2 = ___
6 + 2 = ___	3 + 6 = ___	2 + 7 = ___

(e)

5 + 2 = ___	2 + 7 = ___	1 + 5 = ___
6 + 3 = ___	3 + 4 = ___	1 + 8 = ___
2 + 1 = ___	4 + 4 = ___	5 + 3 = ___
2 + 4 = ___	3 + 6 = ___	1 + 7 = ___

2. For this final set, time yourself again if you want to compare how much you've improved since your first round on page 67!

2 + 2 = ___	3 + 6 = ___
3 + 2 = ___	5 + 3 = ___
6 + 3 = ___	4 + 4 = ___
2 + 5 = ___	4 + 5 = ___
6 + 2 = ___	4 + 3 = ___
3 + 3 = ___	2 + 4 = ___

Time:

3. Back to some algebra. Pay attention to the 'type' of things you're adding together, and make sure you include that in your answer.

a)

3💧 + 5💧 = _____   1★ + 8★ = _____   5💧 + 2💧 = _____

7★ + 2★ = _____   3a + 3a = _____   6a + 1a = _____

2a + 3a = _____   4💧 + 1💧 = _____   3★ + 6★ = _____

4x + 5x = _____   1x + 7x = _____   2💧 + 2💧 = _____

b)

1x + 4x = _____   6💧 + 2💧 = _____   3★ + 4★ = _____

5★ + 3★ = _____   7a + 2a = _____   5x + 1x = _____

2💧 + 6💧 = _____   3★ + 3★ = _____   8a + 1a = _____

7a + 1a = _____   1x + 5x = _____   2💧 + 7💧 = _____

c)

4★ + 5★ = _____   1a + 8a = _____   3a + 5a = _____

3a + 2a = _____   2💧 + 6💧 = _____   4★ + 4★ = _____

1💧 + 1💧 = _____   5x + 2x = _____   7x + 2x = _____

8★ + 1★ = _____   4💧 + 3💧 = _____   2★ + 1★ = _____

d)

6💧 + 3💧 = _____   7a + 1a = _____   3★ + 3★ = _____

4x + 4x = _____   2★ + 4★ = _____   1💧 + 8💧 = _____

2★ + 3★ = _____   5💧 + 2💧 = _____   6x + 2x = _____

1💧 + 5💧 = _____   2★ + 7★ = _____   2a + 4a = _____

ANSWERS: Mastering basic facts under 10

Page 67

1.
9	5
7	8
6	4
3	2

2.
8	9
5	8
6	6
9	7
8	7
9	4

Page 74

3.
(a)
5	8	9
9	8	5
6	4	5
9	9	7

(b)
9	3	8
9	5	7
8	7	9
7	8	6

ANSWERS: Mastering basic facts under 10

Page 74

(c)

7	9	7
9	7	6
8	9	7
4	8	5

Page 75

(d)

8	9	7
9	7	4
8	6	7
8	9	9

(e)

7	9	6
9	7	9
3	8	8
6	9	8

2.

4	9
5	8
9	8
7	9
8	7
6	6

ANSWERS: Mastering basic facts under 10

Page 76

(a)

8💧	9★	7💧
9★	6a	7a
5a	5💧	9★
9x	8x	4💧

(b)

5x	8💧	7★
8★	9a	6x
8💧	6★	9a
8a	6x	9💧

(c)

9★	9a	8a
5a	8💧	8★
2💧	7x	9x
9★	7💧	3★

(d)

9💧	8a	6★
8x	6★	9💧
5★	7💧	8x
6💧	9★	6a

Understanding word problems

Here are some situations where you'd use addition to solve problems. They're already solved for you, so don't worry about the answers.

Do have a good look at the kinds of questions they are, especially the difference between addition and subtraction.

1. Fill in the '___' spaces to create the number equations.

a)

You've already saved $2 and then you save another $3 this week.

How much money do you have in total?

This question is asking:

_____ + _____ = 5

b)

You have $50 in your savings and then you save another $65 this week.

How much money do you have in total?

This question is asking:

_____ + _____ = $115

c)

At the start of the month your savings are $1500. After the first fortnight* you have saved $300 more, and then after the second fortnight you have saved $400 more. (*A fortnight is 2 weeks.)

How much do you have saved at the end of the month?

This question is asking:

_____ + _____ + _____ = $2200

80

d

You have 3 carrots in your fridge at home, and you buy another 4 at the market.

How many carrots do you have in total?

This question is asking:

_____ + _____ = 7

e

A carrot farmer is trying to break the world record for the world's biggest carrot. Last week, he planted 15 giant carrot seeds. This week, he planted 25 more.

How many giant carrots did he plant in total?

This question is asking:

_____ + _____ = 40

f

You make and sell carrot cakes for a living. You have 600 carrots in your fridge at work, and you buy another 950 at the market.

How many carrots do you have in total?

This question is asking:

_____ + _____ = 1550

g) You're going on a trip to the beach. Your first bus ticket will cost you $4, and then your second bus ticket will cost you $5. How much will your bus tickets cost you in total?

This question is asking:

_____ + _____ = 9

h) You're going on holiday. Your first plane ticket will cost you $320, and then your second plane ticket will cost you $290. How much will your plane tickets cost you in total?

This question is asking:

_____ + _____ = $610

2. Here are two examples where you'd use **subtraction**:

a) If you had 9 carrots and used 6 of them in a week, how many carrots would you have leftover at the end of that week?

This question is asking:

_____ − _____ = 3

b) If you had a total of $396 in savings, and then spent $380 of it on a laptop, how much money would you have left?

This question is asking:

_____ − _____ = 16

3. Circle addition or subtraction under each word problem. Then figure out the equation you would need to solve to find the answer.

a) You saved $17 last week, and then $20 this week. How much did you save in total over the two weeks?

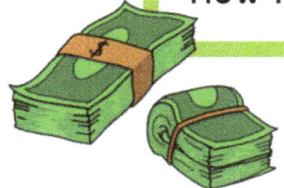

This question is **(addition)/subtraction**.
Equation:
17 + 20 = $37

b) You had $80 in your piggy bank, and then you spent $15 dollars on your friend's birthday present. How much money does your piggy bank have left?

This question is **addition/subtraction**.
Equation:
_____ = $95

c) You're going on a tropical holiday. Your accommodation costs $5600, and your plane tickets cost $950. How much will this holiday cost you in total?

This question is **addition/subtraction**.
Equation:
_____ = $6550

d) You're building a sandcastle on your tropical holiday. You build 17 towers, but then huge waves crash in and knock over 5 of them. How many towers are still left standing?

This question is **addition/subtraction**.
Equation:
_____ = 12

ANSWERS: Understanding word problems

Page 80

1.

a. $2 savings plus another $3 in savings is written as 2 + 3 = $5
b. $50 savings plus another $65 in savings is written as 50 + 65 = $115
c. $1500 savings plus $300 more savings plus another $400 is written as: $1500 + 300 + 400 = $2200

Page 81:

d. 3 carrots in your fridge plus another 4 from the market is written as 3 + 4 = 7
e. 15 carrots seeds plus another 25 carrots seeds is written as 15 + 25 = 40
f. 600 carrots in your fridge plus 950 from the market is written as 600 + 950 = 1550

Page 82:

g. First $4 plane ticket plus second $5 plane ticket is written as 4 + 5 = 9
h. First $320 plane ticket plus second $290 plane ticket is written as 320 + 290 = $410

2.

a. 9 carrots minus 6 carrots used up is written as 9 − 6 = 3
b. $396 in savings minus $380 spent on a laptop is written as 396 − 380 = $16

ANSWERS: Understanding word problems

Page 83

<u>3.</u>

a. ADDITION: $17 saved last week plus $20 saved this week is written as <u>17 + 20 =</u> $37

b. SUBTRACTION: $80 in your piggy bank minus $15 spent on the present is written as <u>80 − 15 =</u> $65

c. ADDITION: $5600 accommodation costs plus $950 plane tickets is written as <u>5600 + 950 =</u> $6550

d. SUBTRACTION: 17 towers minus 5 knocked over by the waves is written as <u>17 − 5 =</u> 2

Pairs to 10

1. For any kind of math to go smoothly, we want to have a really strong foundation. You did a lot of work focusing on the numbers under 10. Now, answer these questions about the number 10.

Let's say you have 10 apples in your basket.

Doris only has 4 apples in her basket.

a) How many more apples does Doris need to fill her basket to 10?

_____ more apples

b) What if she had 7 apples?

_____ more apples

c) What if she had 3 apples?

_____ more apples

Remember how we can swap our adding numbers around?

7 + 3 = 10

and...

3 + 7 = 10

Well, instead of remembering both that 3 + 7 = 10 AND 7 + 3 = 10, you can just remember the pair of (7 & 3) makes 10.

<u>2</u>. Here's all the combinations to make 10 that you'll ever need to know:

____ & ____

____ & ____

____ & ____

____ & ____

____ & ____

____ & ____

87

To recap: at first, it might seem like you have to remember all of...

0 + 10 = 10	1 + 9 = 10
2 + 8 = 10	3 + 7 = 10
4 + 6 = 10	5 + 5 = 10
6 + 4 = 10	7 + 3 = 10
8 + 2 = 10	9 + 1 = 10
10 + 0 = 10	which is quite a lot ...

... but actually ...

... since half of these are just the same equation with the adding numbers swapped, all you really have to remember is:

0 and 10 = 10	3 and 7 = 10
1 and 9 = 10	4 and 6 = 10
2 and 8 = 10	5 and 5 = 10

Learn these pairs, and you'll know all the possible combinations to 10.

<u>3.</u> Match each star up to their buddy to make 10!

If there's ever a time when you don't have diagrams and you need help, use your fingers!

You just happen to have the perfect tool for learning pairs to 10 on your body! You may have been told that using your fingers is bad, but it's the easiest way everyone uses to start learning their basic facts.

Once you've gone over your basic facts a few times, your brain will know how to do them without using your fingers at all.

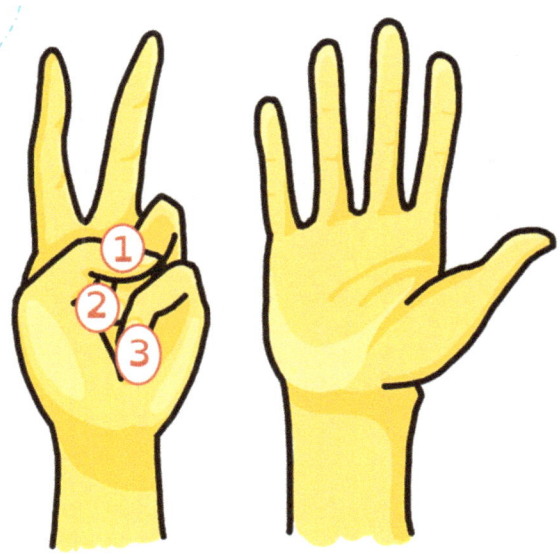

A full set of 10 fingers

3 + ___ = 10

Take the number you're trying to find the pair with, and put that number of fingers **down**.

3 fingers down

3 + 7 = 10

Count how many fingers are left, and that's your answer.

3 + 7 = 10

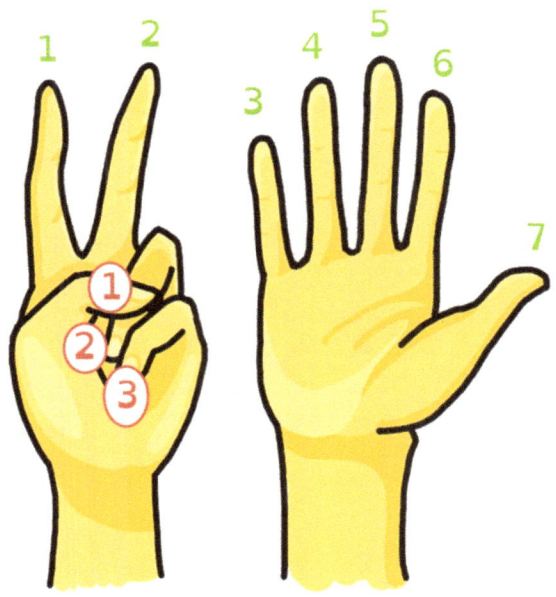

7 fingers still up

Try it out yourself!

Or, we can use stories to help us remember our pairs to 10.
Since 10 is a fizzy drink and donut, all these stories are about junk food.

Let's look at the pair 1 and 9.

  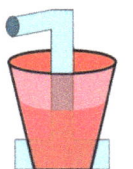

While wearing the Magician's hat, Goldfish had the fizzy drink and donut.

Let's look at the pair 2 and 8.

  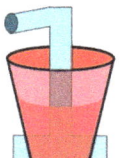

Swan and Honeybee had a snack together. Swan ate the donut, and Honeybee drank the fizzy drink.

Let's look at the pair 3 and 7.

 &  =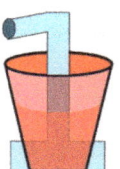

Someone threw a Boomerang at Snake while he was eating junk food (I wonder who it was ...)

Let's look at the pair 4 and 6.

Flamingo found a whistle accidentally baked in her donut.

For the pair 5 and 5:

Magician used magic to clone himself so he wouldn't be lonely and have to eat his donut and drink by himself.

And for the pair 10 and 0:

To get a donut and a drink, all you need is a donut and a drink. You don't need to add anything else!

4. Time yourself doing this set, then review.
Revise the stories of any questions you get stuck on, or write/chant the full equation out a few times. Then do the star activity and try the next set and see if your time and/or accuracy improves!

a

1 + ____ = 10	3 + ____ = 10
4 + ____ = 10	7 + ____ = 10
5 + ____ = 10	2 + ____ = 10
8 + ____ = 10	6 + ____ = 10
0 + ____ = 10	9 + ____ = 10

Time:

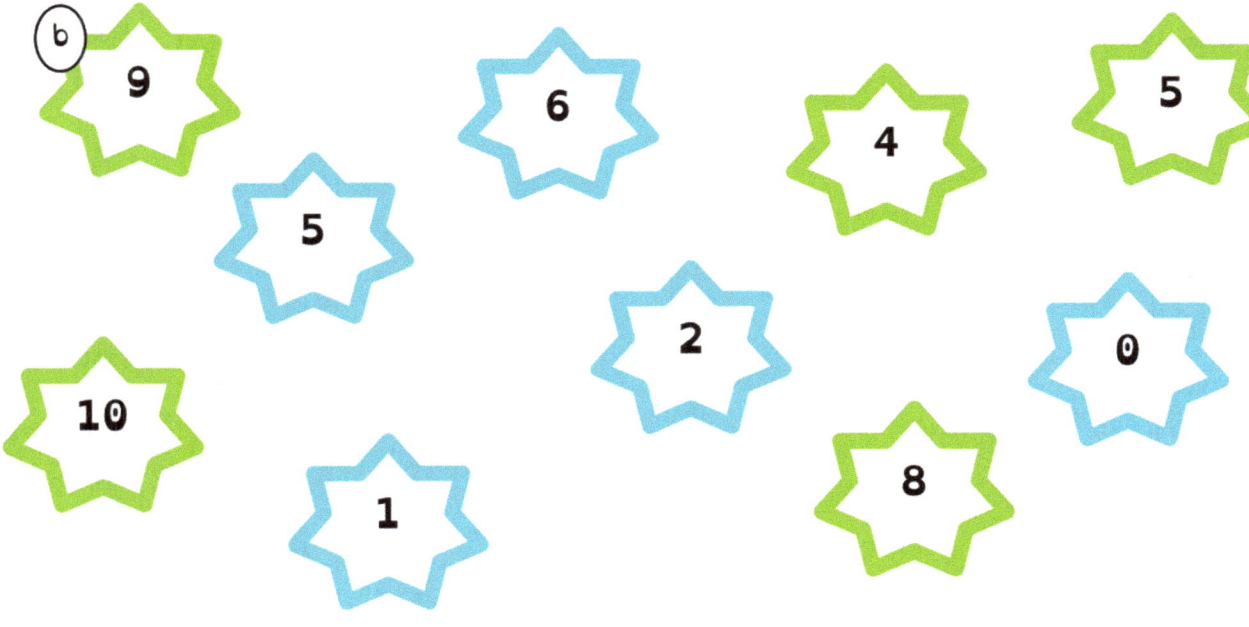

b

c

3 + ____ = 10	9 + ____ = 10
8 + ____ = 10	5 + ____ = 10
4 + ____ = 10	0 + ____ = 10
7 + ____ = 10	1 + ____ = 10
2 + ____ = 10	6 + ____ = 10

Time:

5. Match these stars up to their pairs to make 10. But this time, don't be thrown off by the distractions! Not all the stars will have buddies.

6. And try these questions again!

a)

4 + ___ = 10	0 + ___ = 10
9 + ___ = 10	1 + ___ = 10
3 + ___ = 10	6 + ___ = 10
2 + ___ = 10	7 + ___ = 10
5 + ___ = 10	8 + ___ = 10

Time:

c)

1 + ___ = 10	5 + ___ = 10
6 + ___ = 10	2 + ___ = 10
3 + ___ = 10	0 + ___ = 10
4 + ___ = 10	9 + ___ = 10
8 + ___ = 10	7 + ___ = 10

Time:

ANSWERS: Pairs to 10

Page 86

<u>1.</u>

a. 6 more apples

b. 3 more apples

c. 7 more apples

Page 87

<u>2.</u>

10 & 0
9 & 1
8 & 2
7 & 3
6 & 4
5 & 5

Page 88

<u>3.</u>

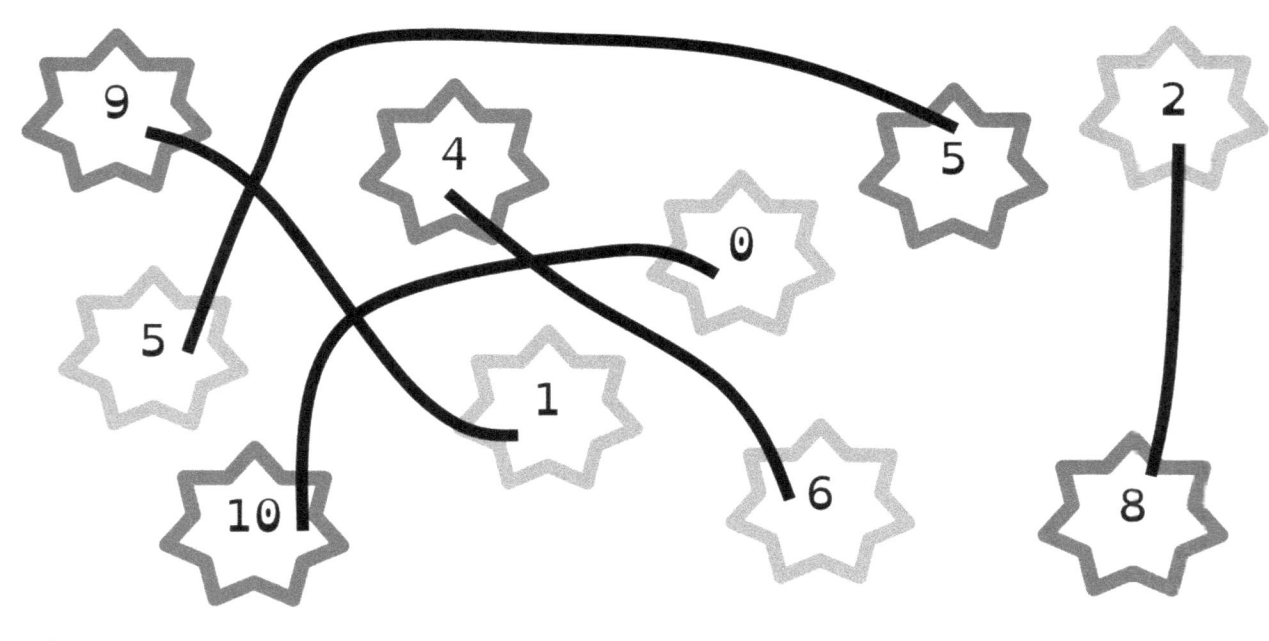

ANSWERS: Pairs to 10

Page 93

<u>4.</u>

a.

9	7
6	3
5	8
2	4
10	1

b.

9 — 1
6 — 4
5 — 5
10 — 0
2 — 8

c.

7	1
2	5
6	10
3	9
8	4

ANSWERS: Pairs to 10

Page 94

<u>5.</u> As long as you've linked the stars up to the same answer, you can mark yourself as correct!

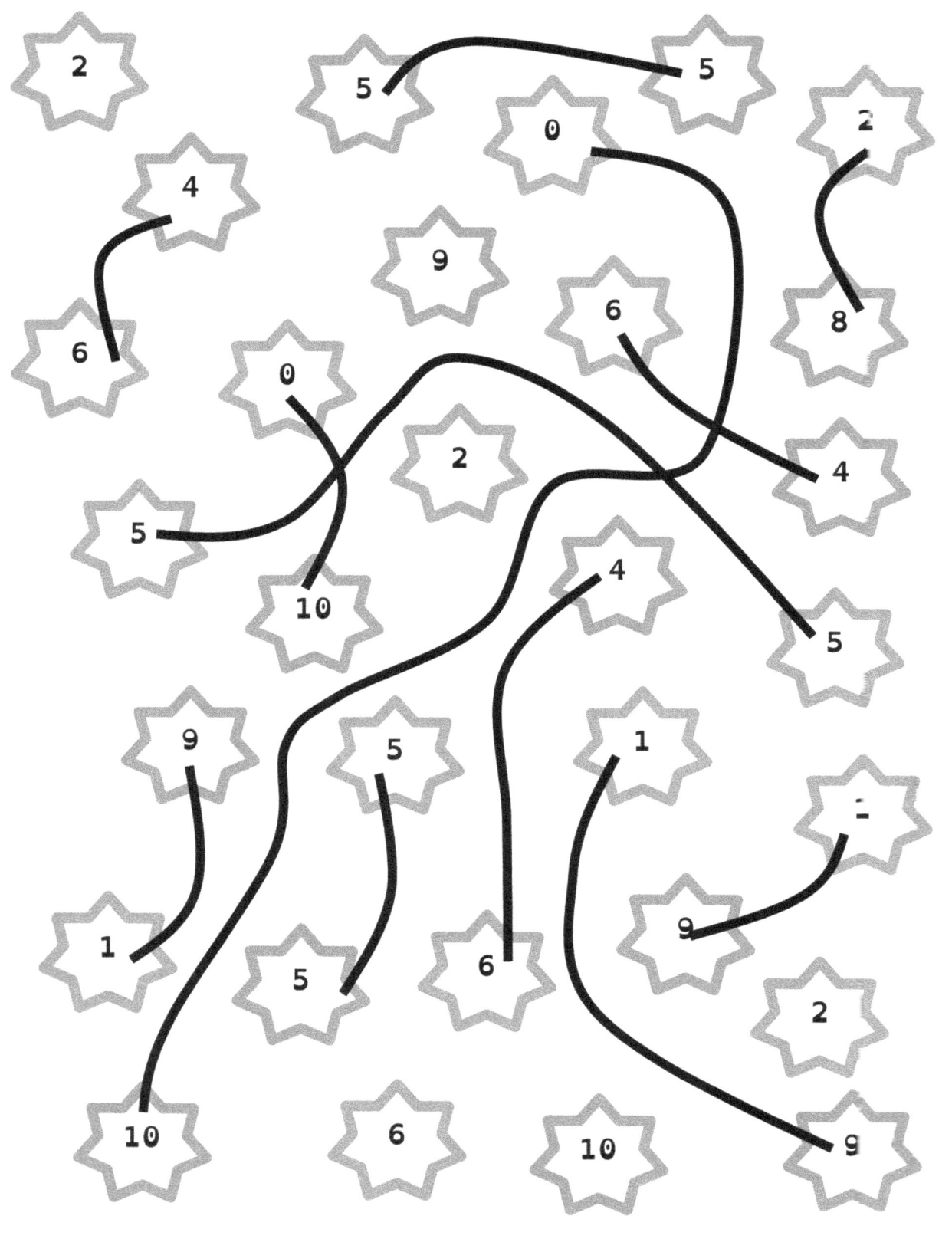

ANSWERS: Pairs to 10

Page 95

4.

a.
6	10
1	9
7	4
8	3
5	8

b.
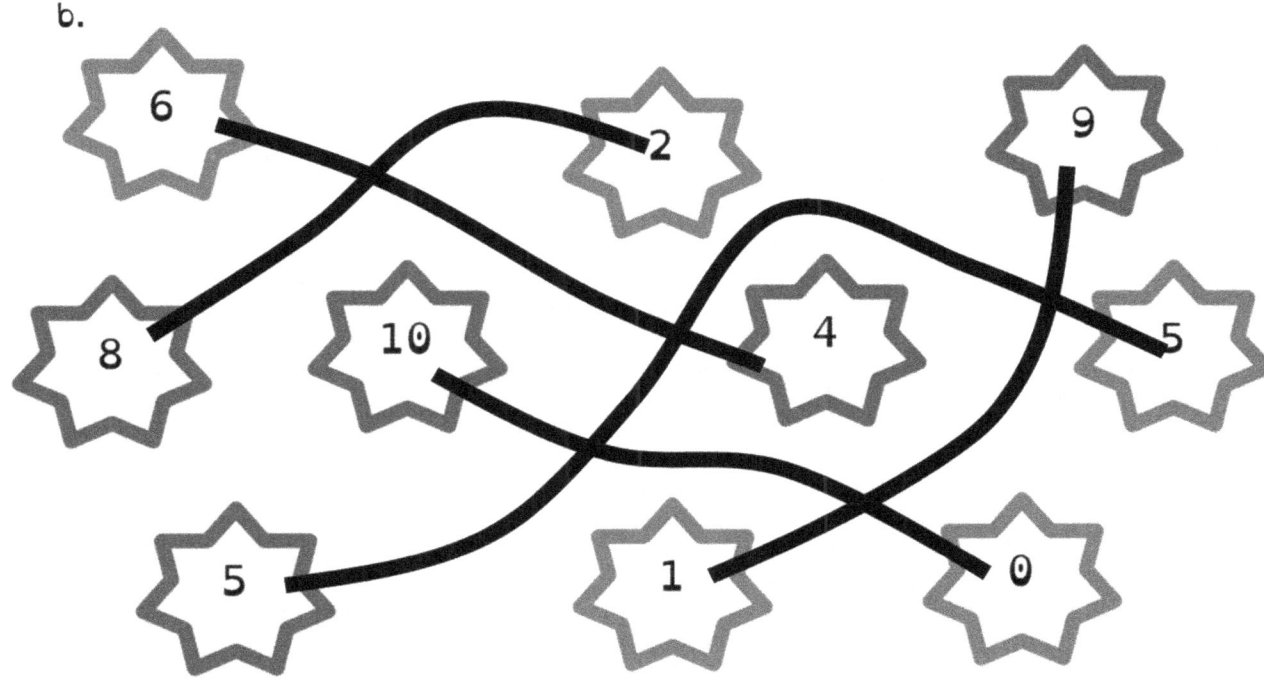

c.
9	5
4	8
7	10
6	1
2	3

Using pairs to 10 for higher additions

Once you know your pairs to 10, it's very easy to learn your pairs to 20, and any other multiple of 10!

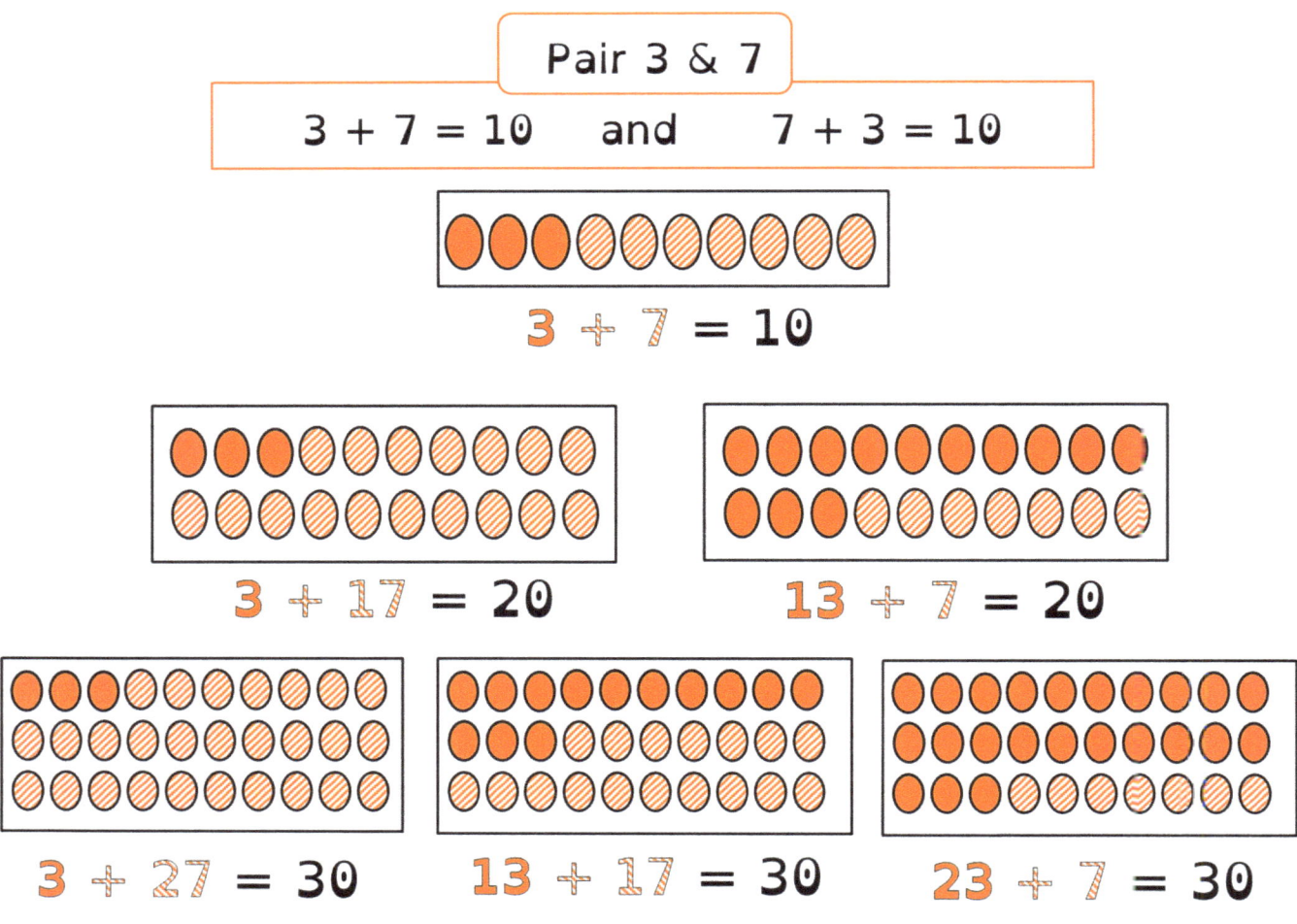

And this pattern continues, but let's get you to discover this for yourself. Grab (or make) a little counter, or just use your finger, and let's go exploring the hundreds square.

Follow the diagram and steps below to see how we use the hundred square.

13 + ____ = 50

1	2	3	4	5	6	7	8	9	10
11	12	13	14	15	16	17	18	19	20
21	22	23	24	25	26	27	28	29	30
31	32	33	34	35	36	37	38	39	40
41	42	43	44	45	46	47	48	49	50
51	52	53	54	55	56	57	58	59	60

Step 1. Calculate how much it will take to reach the end of the row (the nearest tidy number).

13 + 7 = 20

Step 2. Calculate how many rows down you need to jump to reach the final answer. Each jump down is +10, so three jumps is +30.

20 + 30 = 50

Step 3. Add up all the jumps you've made. Here, we jumped 7, and then 30.

13 + 7 + 30 = 50

13 + 37 = 50

1. Your turn! Use the green dots to help you.

62 + ____ = 90

51	52	53	54	55	56	57	58	59	60
61	62	63	64	65	66	67	68	69	70
71	72	73	74	75	76	77	78	79	80
81	82	83	84	85	86	87	88	89	90
91	92	93	94	95	96	97	98	99	100

Step 1. Calculate how much it will take to reach the end of the row to get to the nearest tidy number.

a) 62 + ____ = 70

Step 2. Calculate how many columns down you need to jump to reach the final answer.

b) 70 + ____ = 90

Step 3. Add up all the jumps, then write the answer on the equation at the top.

c) 62 + ____ + ____ = 90

2. Try these two questions now (you can use the grid above to help you):

a) 54 + ____ = 80

b) 83 + ____ = 100

3. Give these questions a go:

a) 4 + ____ = 10

b) 4 + ____ = 20

c) 24 + ____ = 30

d) 24 + ____ = 40

e) 54 + ____ = 60

f) 54 + ____ = 80

g) 84 + ____ = 90

h) 84 + ____ = 100

1	2	3	4	5	6	7	8	9	10
11	12	13	14	15	16	17	18	19	20
21	22	23	24	25	26	27	28	29	30
31	32	33	34	35	36	37	38	39	40
41	42	43	44	45	46	47	48	49	50
51	52	53	54	55	56	57	58	59	60
61	62	63	64	65	66	67	68	69	70
71	72	73	74	75	76	77	78	79	80
81	82	83	84	85	86	87	88	89	90
91	92	93	94	95	96	97	98	99	100

4. Let's do a few more:

a) 2 + _____ = 10

b) 12 + _____ = 20

c) 23 + _____ = 30

d) 23 + _____ = 40

e) 54 + _____ = 60

f) 54 + _____ = 80

g) 87 + _____ = 90

h) 87 + _____ = 100

1	2	3	4	5	6	7	8	9	10
11	12	13	14	15	16	17	18	19	20
21	22	23	24	25	26	27	28	29	30
31	32	33	34	35	36	37	38	39	40
41	42	43	44	45	46	47	48	49	50
51	52	53	54	55	56	57	58	59	60
61	62	63	64	65	66	67	68	69	70
71	72	73	74	75	76	77	78	79	80
81	82	83	84	85	86	87	88	89	90
91	92	93	94	95	96	97	98	99	100

5. Here's a final set of questions. See if you can do them without the grid!

a) 1 + ____ = 10

b) 11 + ____ = 20

c) 24 + ____ = 40

d) 24 + ____ = 50

e) 55 + ____ = 70

f) 55 + ____ = 80

g) 86 + ____ = 90

h) 86 + ____ = 100

1	2	3	4	5	6	7	8	9	10
11	12	13	14	15	16	17	18	19	20
21	22	23	24	25	26	27	28	29	30
31	32	33	34	35	36	37	38	39	40
41	42	43	44	45	46	47	48	49	50
51	52	53	54	55	56	57	58	59	60
61	62	63	64	65	66	67	68	69	70
71	72	73	74	75	76	77	78	79	80
81	82	83	84	85	86	87	88	89	90
91	92	93	94	95	96	97	98	99	100

6. Your turn, all by yourself now.

a) 14 + ___ = 20

b) 13 + ___ = 20

c) 12 + ___ = 20

d) 16 + ___ = 30

e) 27 + ___ = 40

f) 18 + ___ = 40

g) 11 + ___ = 40

h) 15 + ___ = 40

i) 19 + ___ = 80

j) 12 + ___ = 50

k) 21 + ___ = 80

l) 14 + ___ = 100

7. Let's quickly go over our pairs to 10 again.

3 + ___ = 10	8 + ___ = 10	5 + ___ = 10
9 + ___ = 10	7 + ___ = 10	2 + ___ = 10
4 + ___ = 10	1 + ___ = 10	6 + ___ = 10

8. Now, let's use them to shortcut our pairs to 20.

a

8 + ___ = 20	6 + ___ = 20	3 + ___ = 20
2 + ___ = 20	7 + ___ = 20	9 + ___ = 20

b

14 + ___ = 20	18 + ___ = 20	10 + ___ = 20
17 + ___ = 20	12 + ___ = 20	11 + ___ = 20

c

1 + ___ = 20	5 + ___ = 20	17 + ___ = 20
3 + ___ = 20	16 + ___ = 20	8 + ___ = 20
12 + ___ = 20	3 + ___ = 20	19 + ___ = 20

9. Now, you can figure out the answers for any tidy numbers. Go across.

a

3 + ___ = 10	3 + ___ = 20	3 + ___ = 30
3 + ___ = 40	3 + ___ = 50	3 + ___ = 60
3 + ___ = 70	3 + ___ = 80	3 + ___ = 90
3 + ___ = 100	3 + ___ = 110	3 + ___ = 120

b

2 + ___ = 10	8 + ___ = 50	5 + ___ = 30
9 + ___ = 60	1 + ___ = 40	6 + ___ = 80
4 + ___ = 70	3 + ___ = 80	0 + ___ = 30
10 + ___ = 100	7 + ___ = 140	3 + ___ = 120

ANSWERS: Using pairs to 10 for higher additions

Page 102

<u>1.</u>

a. 62 + <u>8</u> = 70

b. 70 + <u>20</u> = 90

c. 62 + <u>8</u> + <u>20</u> = 90 so 62 + <u>28</u> = 90

<u>2.</u>

a. 54 + <u>26</u> = 80 (first add 6 then 20)

b. 83 + <u>17</u> = 100 (first add 7 then 10)

Page 103

<u>3.</u>
a. 6   b. 16   c. 6   d. 16   e. 6   f. 26   g. 6   h. 16

Page 104

<u>4.</u>
a. 8   b. 8   c. 7   d. 17   e. 6   f. 26   g. 3   h. 13

Page 105

<u>5.</u>
a. 9   b. 9   c. 16   d. 26   e. 15   f. 25   g. 4   h. 14

ANSWERS: Using pairs to 10 for higher additions

Page 106

6.
a. 6	b. 7	c. 8
d. 14	e. 13	f. 22
g. 29	h. 25	i. 61
j. 38	k. 59	l. 86

Page 107

7.
7	2	5
1	3	8
6	9	4

8.

a.
12	14	17
18	13	11

b.
6	2	10
3	8	9

ANSWERS: Using pairs to 10 for higher additions

Page 107

8.

c.
19	15	3
17	4	12
8	17	1

9.

a.
7	17	27
37	47	57
67	77	87
97	107	117

b.
8	42	25
51	39	74
66	77	30
90	133	117

Shortcuts for adding 10 (and numbers close to 10)

Here's a shortcut for adding 10s.

Do you notice a pattern?

5 + 10 = 15

15 + 10 = 25

25 + 10 = 35

35 + 10 = 45

45 + 10 = 55

55 + 10 = 65

If you don't see a pattern, this might help:

Digit in the tens place (1)

Digit in the tens place (1)

15 + 10 = 25

Added together (1 + 1 = 2)

Digit in the tens place (4)

Digit in the tens place (1)

45 + 10 = 55

Added together (4 + 1 = 5)

1. Keep this pattern going!

3 + 10 = 13

13 + 10 = 23

a) 23 + 10 = _____

b) 33 + 10 = _____

c) 43 + 10 = _____

2. Watch out in these ones:

a) 7 + 10 = _____

b) 37 + 10 = _____

c) 67 + 10 = _____

d) 27 + 10 = _____

e) 87 + 10 = _____

3. Two more random questions:

a) 59 + 10 = _____

b) 88 + 10 = _____

Here's some examples with bigger numbers:

4<u>1</u>7 + 1<u>0</u> = 4<u>2</u>7

4<u>2</u>7 + 1<u>0</u> = 4<u>3</u>7

4<u>3</u>7 + 1<u>0</u> = 4<u>4</u>7

4<u>4</u>7 + 1<u>0</u> = 4<u>5</u>7

Tip: when adding 9 with 1 (and whenever there are numbers that add up to more than 10) it can be easier to look at two place values.

4<u>9</u>7 + <u>10</u> = <u>50</u>7

<u>49</u>7 + <u>40</u> = <u>53</u>7

4. Give these a try:

a) 217 + 10 = _____

b) 135 + 10 = _____

c) 378 + 10 = _____

d) 924 + 10 = _____

e) 298 + 10 = _____

f) 694 + 10 = _____

(if you get stuck) → (tip: 298 + 10 = 308)

A shortcut for adding 9s

1. Since 9 is just 10 − 1, an easy way to add 9 to another number is to first add 10, and then take away 1.

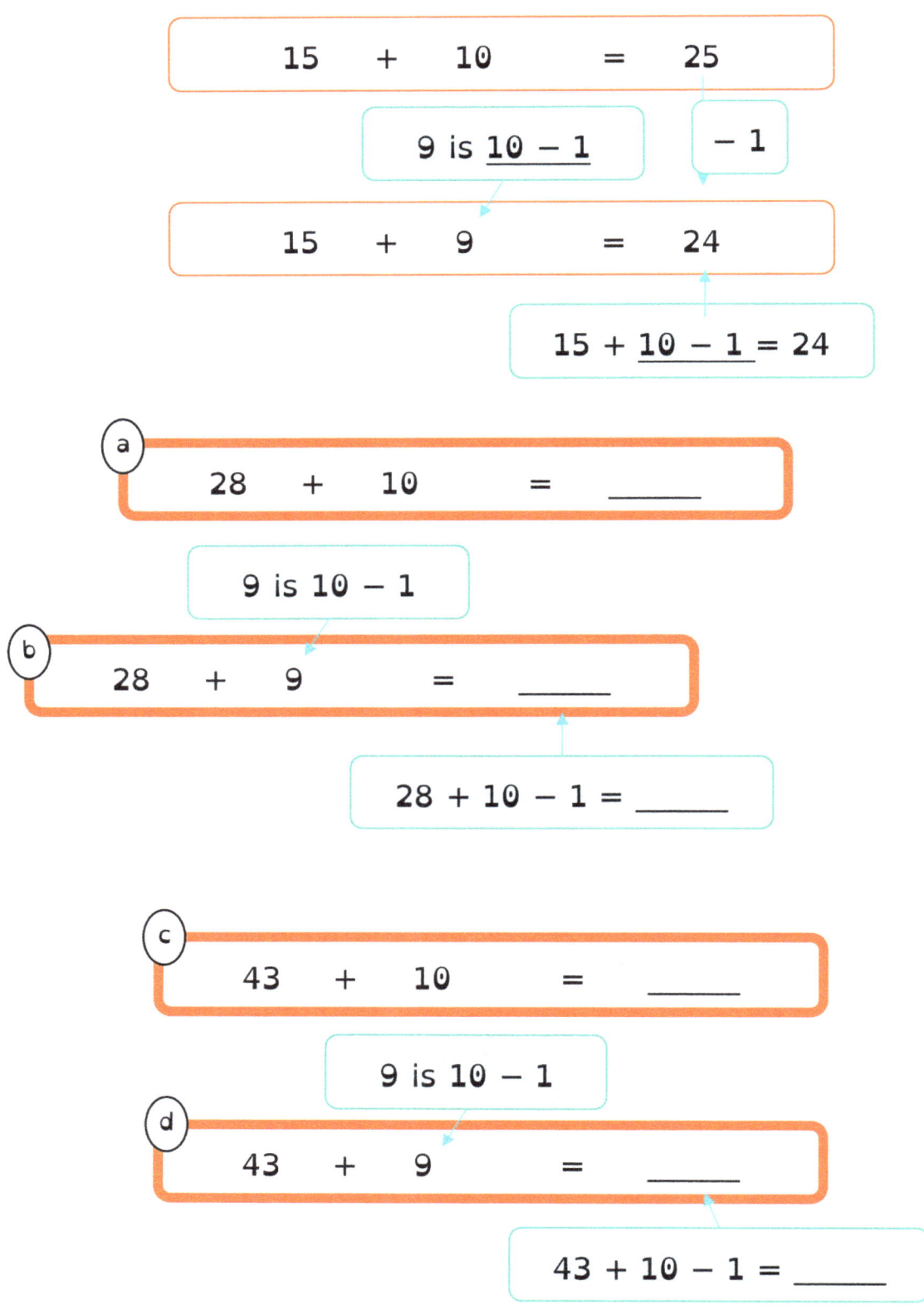

15 + 10 = 25

9 is 10 − 1   − 1

15 + 9 = 24

15 + 10 − 1 = 24

a) 28 + 10 = _____

9 is 10 − 1

b) 28 + 9 = _____

28 + 10 − 1 = _____

c) 43 + 10 = _____

9 is 10 − 1

d) 43 + 9 = _____

43 + 10 − 1 = _____

2. Here's some practice adding 9. Try timing yourself as you do each set and see if your time improves.

a

28 + 9 = _____   45 + 9 = _____

12 + 9 = _____   73 + 9 = _____

37 + 9 = _____   28 + 9 = _____

11 + 9 = _____   52 + 9 = _____

Time:

b

62 + 9 = _____   33 + 9 = _____

26 + 9 = _____   51 + 9 = _____

48 + 9 = _____   15 + 9 = _____

13 + 9 = _____   78 + 9 = _____

Time:

c

42 + 9 = _____   72 + 9 = _____

21 + 9 = _____   46 + 9 = _____

33 + 9 = _____   68 + 9 = _____

59 + 9 = _____   88 + 9 = _____

Time:

A shortcut for adding 8s

1. Since 8 is just 10 − 2, an easy way to add 8 is to first add 10, and then take away 2.

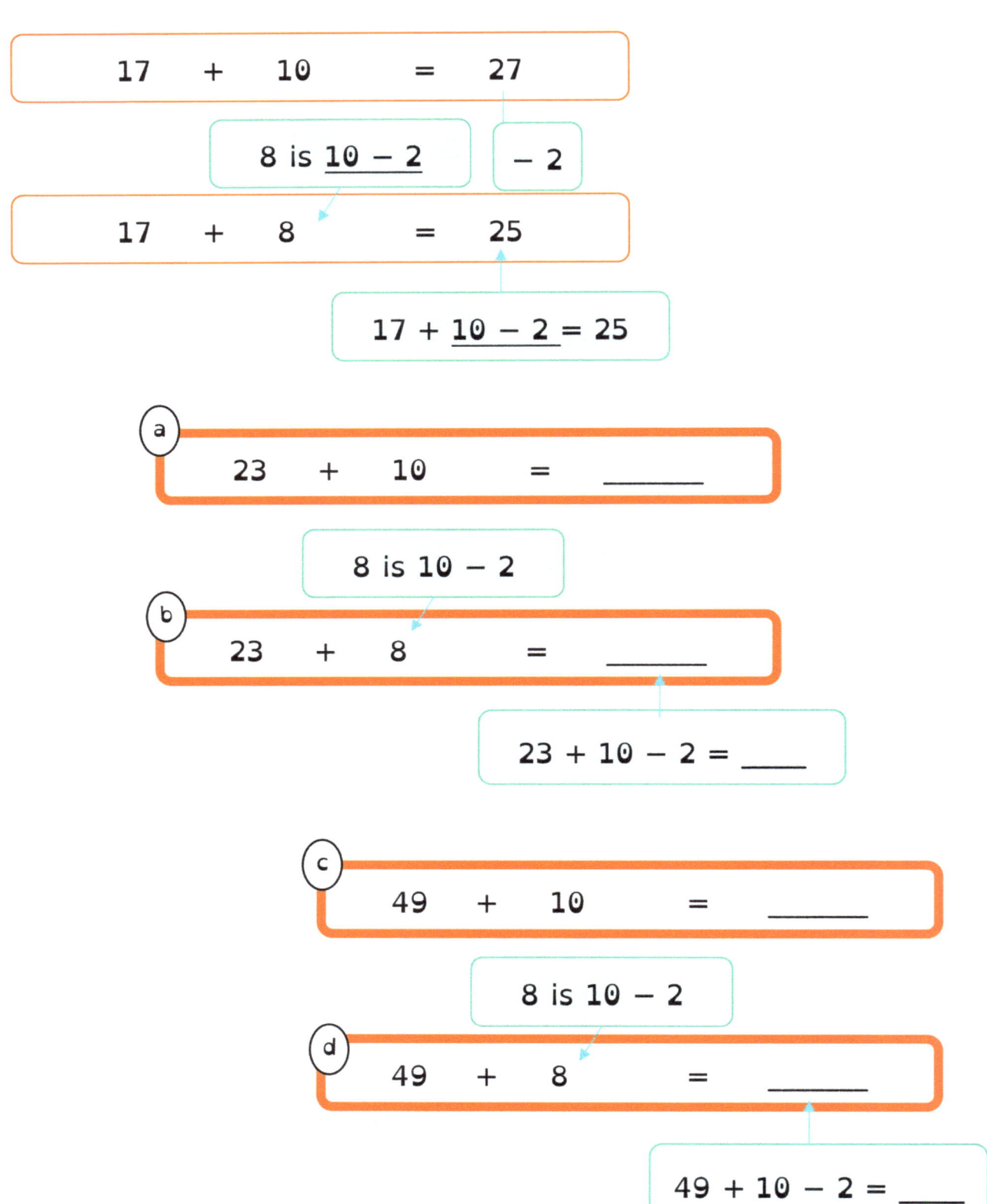

2. Now let's practise adding 8. Try timing yourself as you do each set and see if your time improves.

a)

16 + 8 = _____

34 + 8 = _____

51 + 8 = _____

91 + 8 = _____

47 + 8 = _____

28 + 8 = _____

33 + 8 = _____

86 + 8 = _____

Time:

b)

83 + 8 = _____

39 + 8 = _____

27 + 8 = _____

45 + 8 = _____

99 + 8 = _____

56 + 8 = _____

37 + 8 = _____

13 + 8 = _____

Time:

c)

28 + 8 = _____

55 + 8 = _____

43 + 8 = _____

27 + 8 = _____

12 + 8 = _____

39 + 8 = _____

74 + 8 = _____

26 + 8 = _____

Time:

A shortcut for adding 7s

1. Since 7 is just 10 − 3, an easy way to add 7 is to first add 10, and then take away 3.

15 + 10 = 25

7 is 10 − 3   − 3

15 + 7 = 22

15 + 10 − 3 = 22

a) 29 + 10 = _____

7 is 10 − 3

b) 29 + 7 = _____

29 + 10 − 3 = _____

c) 46 + 10 = _____

7 is 10 − 3

d) 46 + 7 = _____

46 + 10 − 3 = _____

You can also use this method for adding 6 too, but using basic facts is usually faster (we'll learn that soon).

2. Here's some practice adding 7. Try timing yourself as you do each set and see if your time improves.

a)

28 + 7 = _____   45 + 7 = _____

14 + 7 = _____   78 + 7 = _____

37 + 7 = _____   28 + 7 = _____

19 + 7 = _____   52 + 7 = _____

Time:

b)

69 + 7 = _____   33 + 7 = _____

26 + 7 = _____   56 + 7 = _____

48 + 7 = _____   15 + 7 = _____

12 + 7 = _____   78 + 7 = _____

Time:

c)

22 + 7 = _____   79 + 7 = _____

21 + 7 = _____   46 + 7 = _____

83 + 7 = _____   68 + 7 = _____

59 + 7 = _____   18 + 7 = _____

Time:

ANSWERS: Shortcuts for adding 10 and numbers close to 10

Page 112

<u>1.</u>

a. 33   b. 43   c. 53

<u>2.</u>

a. 17   b. 47   c. 77   d. 37   e. 97

<u>3.</u>

a. 69   b. 98

Page 113

<u>4.</u>

a. 227   b. 145   c. 388   d. 934   e. 308   f. 704

Page 114

<u>1.</u>

a. 38   b. 37   c. 53   d. 52

<u>2.</u>
a.

37	44
21	82
46	37
20	61

Page 115

<u>2.</u>
b.

71	42
35	60
57	24
22	87

ANSWERS: Shortcuts for adding 10 and numbers close to 10

Page 115

c.

51	81
30	55
42	77
68	97

Page 116

<u>1.</u>

a. 33   b. 31   c. 59   d. 57

Page 117

<u>2.</u>

a.

24	42
59	99
55	36
41	94

b.

91	47
35	53
107	64
45	21

c.

36	63
51	35
20	47
82	34

ANSWERS: Shortcuts for adding 10 and numbers close to 10

Page 118

1.

a. 39   b. 36   c. 56   d. 53

2.

a.
35	52
21	85
44	35
26	59

b.
76	40
33	63
55	22
19	85

c.
29	86
28	53
90	75
66	25

Doubles and pairs to 20

You've done a great job learning your facts up to 10. Once you master all your facts up to 20, you'll be able to break down and solve any addition problem you like. We'll start with doubles, and then use those to help us with the rest of the equations.

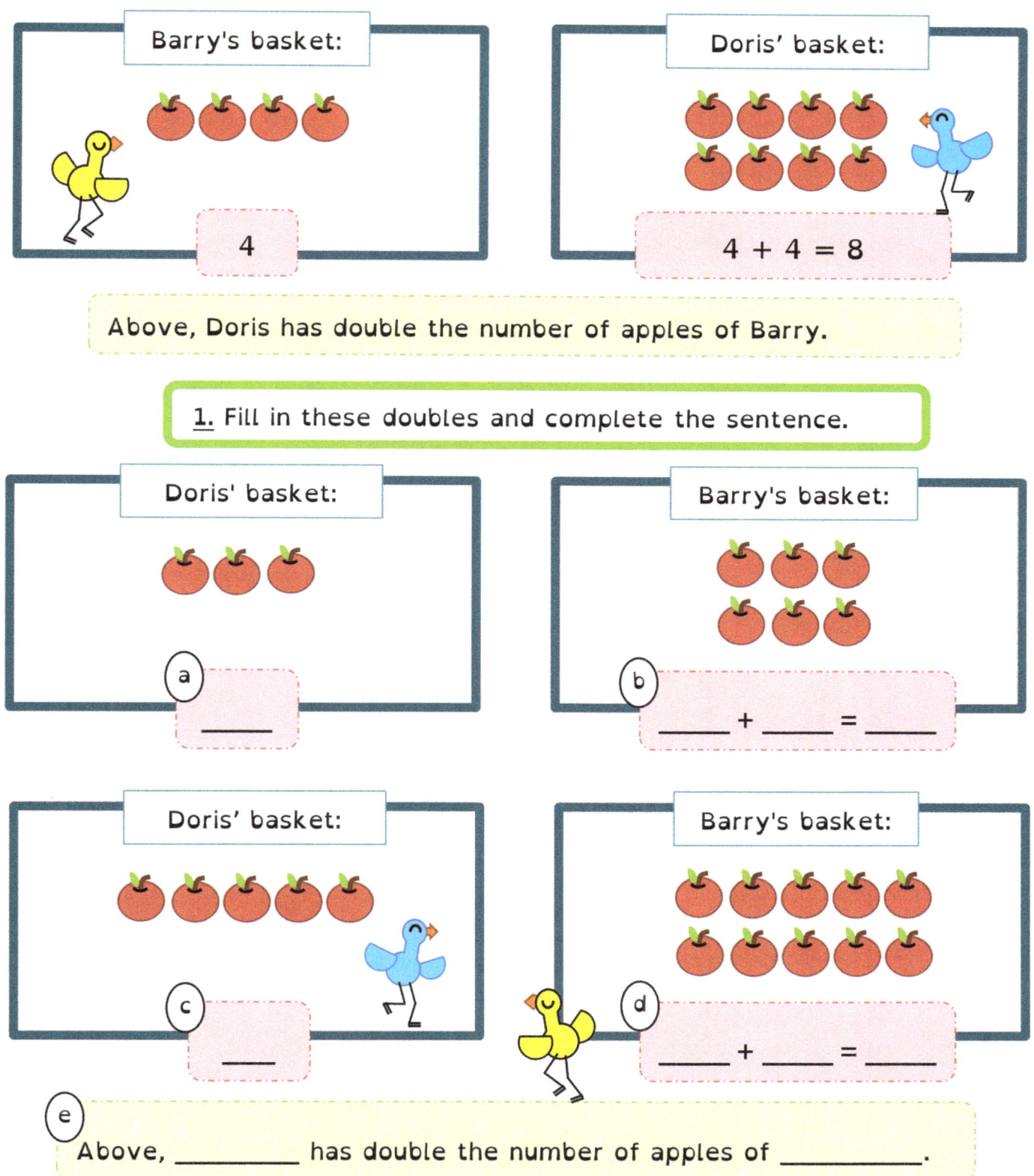

Barry's basket:

4

Doris' basket:

4 + 4 = 8

Above, Doris has double the number of apples of Barry.

1. Fill in these doubles and complete the sentence.

Doris' basket:

a) ____

Barry's basket:

b) ____ + ____ = ____

Doris' basket:

c) ____

Barry's basket:

d) ____ + ____ = ____

e) Above, _____ has double the number of apples of _____.

2. Fill in the gaps (use counting if you need to).

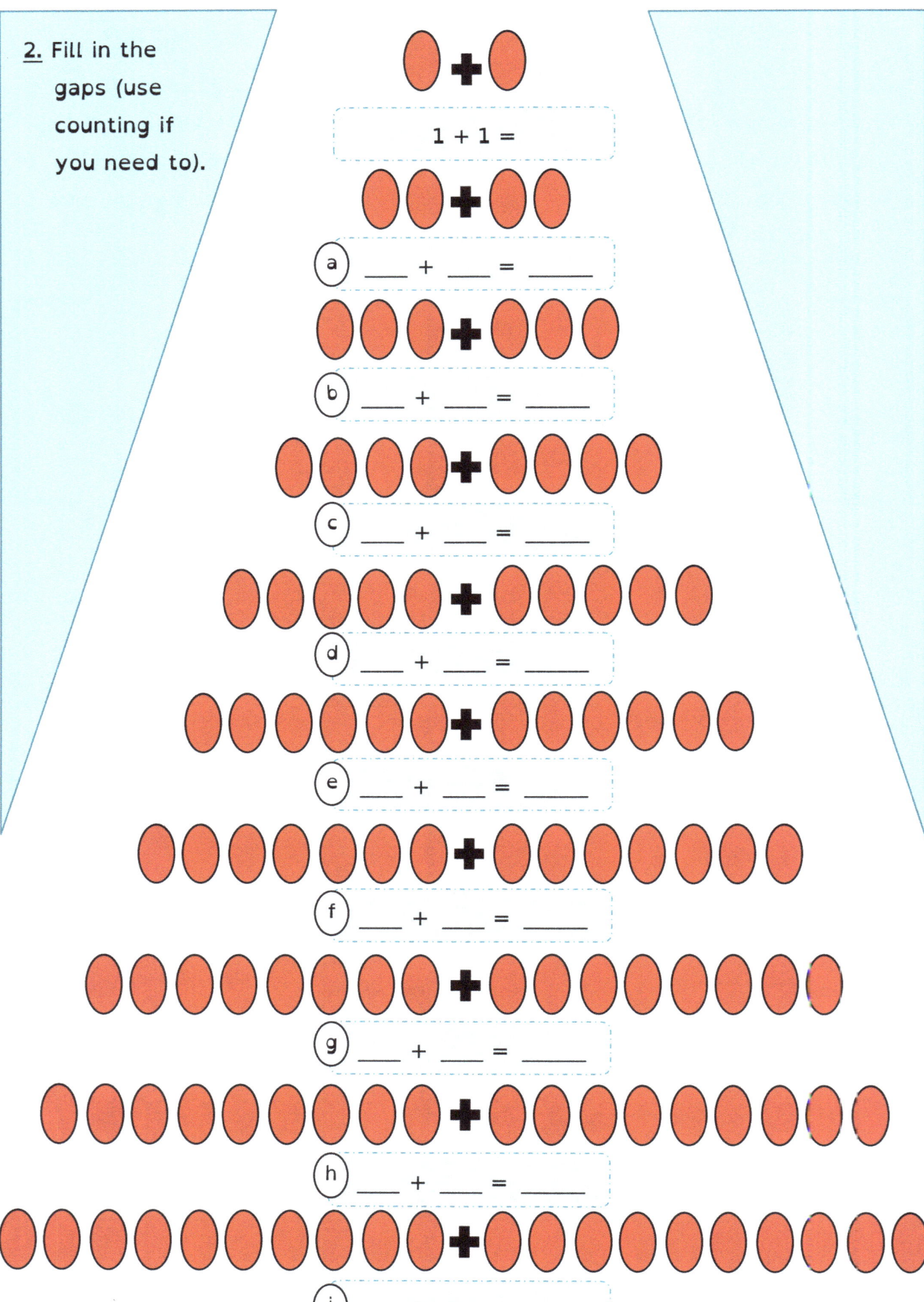

If you like, you can use stories again for these trickier equations. If you need stories for the other doubles too, you can use your own paper.

For the double 6 + 6 = 12

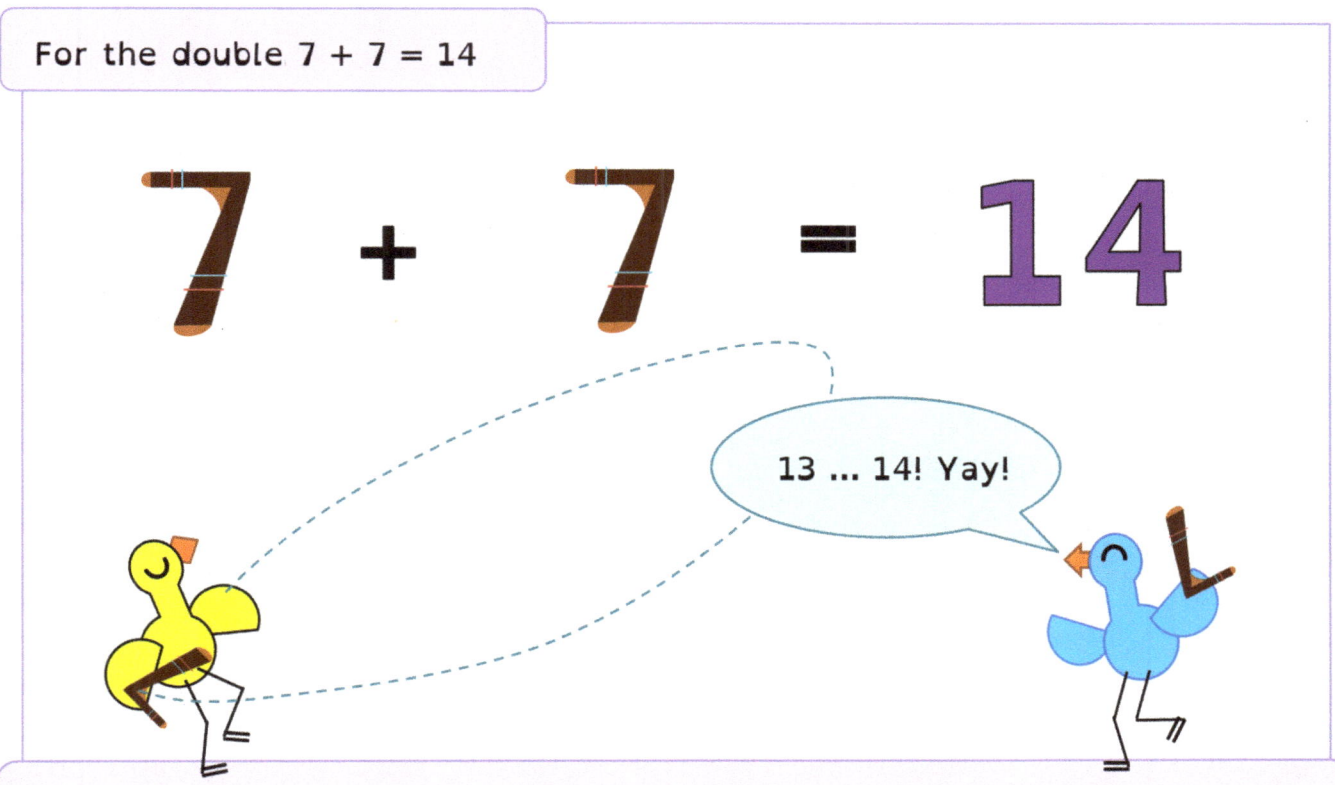

Two whistles blown together was so loud it made 12 birds jump in shock!

For the double 7 + 7 = 14

13 ... 14! Yay!

Barry and Doris played with two boomerangs and caught them 14 times.

Unleash your imagination and create some stories for these doubles:

For the double 8 + 8 = 16

8 + 8 = 16

Story:

For the double 9 + 9 = 18

9 + 9 = 18

Story:

3. Match up these doubles with their answers:

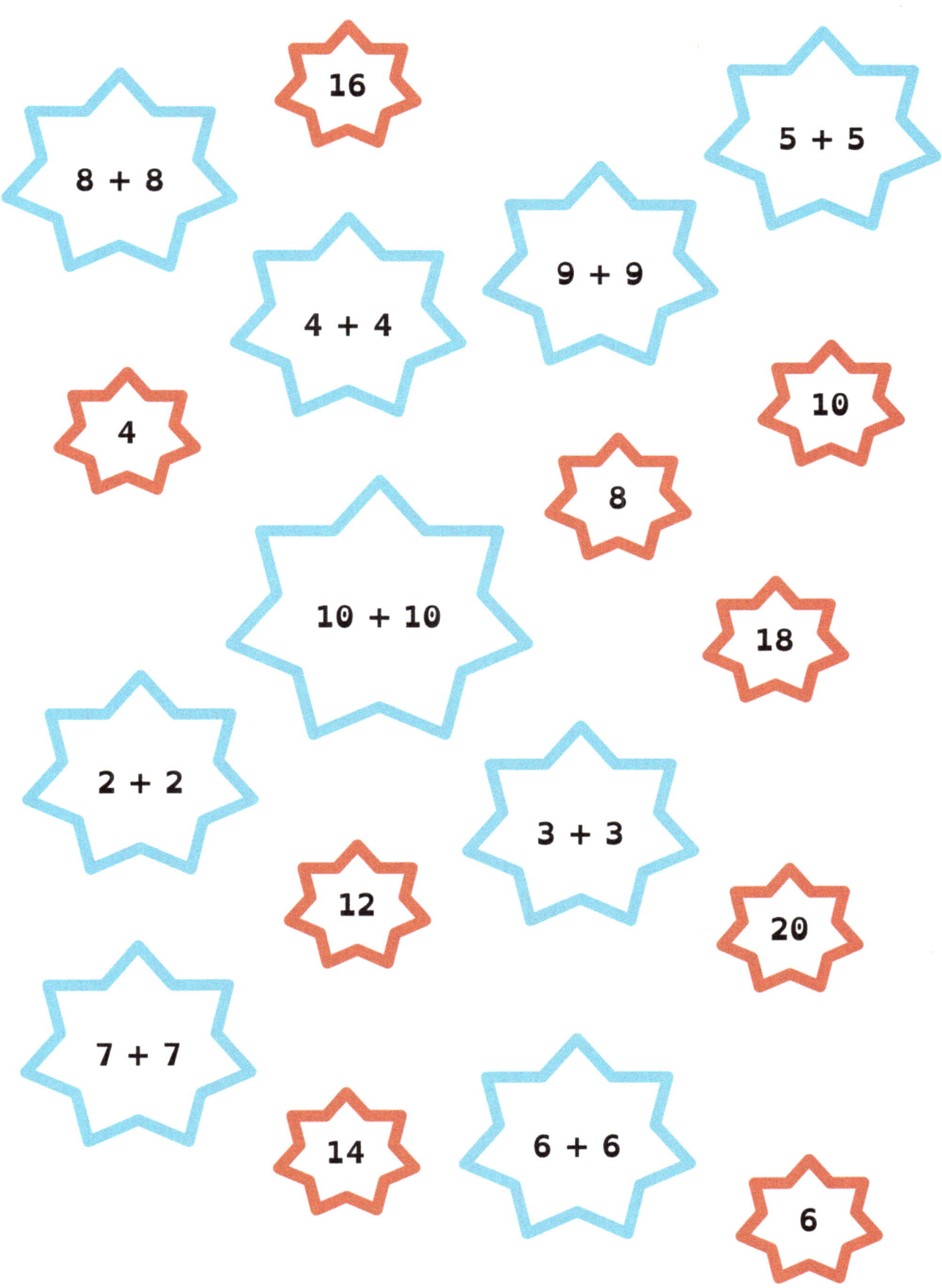

4. Give these a go!

a)

2 + 2 = _____   5 + 5 = _____   1 + 1 = _____

4 + 4 = _____   6 + 6 = _____   9 + 9 = _____

3 + 3 = _____   8 + 8 = _____   7 + 7 = _____

b)

9 + 9 = _____   2 + 2 = _____   6 + 6 = _____

5 + 5 = _____   8 + 8 = _____   7 + 7 = _____

4 + 4 = _____   1 + 1 = _____   3 + 3 = _____

c)

8 + 8 = _____   9 + 9 = _____   5 + 5 = _____

2 + 2 = _____   4 + 4 = _____   1 + 1 = _____

7 + 7 = _____   6 + 6 = _____   5 + 5 = _____

d)

3 + 3 = _____   5 + 5 = _____   7 + 7 = _____

9 + 9 = _____   6 + 6 = _____   4 + 4 = _____

1 + 1 = _____   2 + 2 = _____   8 + 8 = _____

The green numbers below are the doubles which are called even numbers, because they can be split evenly into 2. The odd numbers are those between the even numbers.

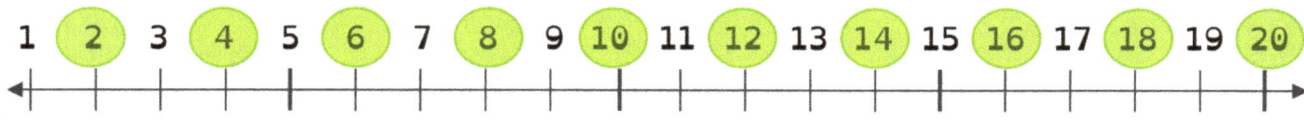

5. Complete the equations below to make odd numbers.

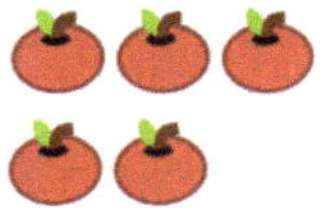

___3___ + ___2___ = ___5___

a) ___ + ___ = ___

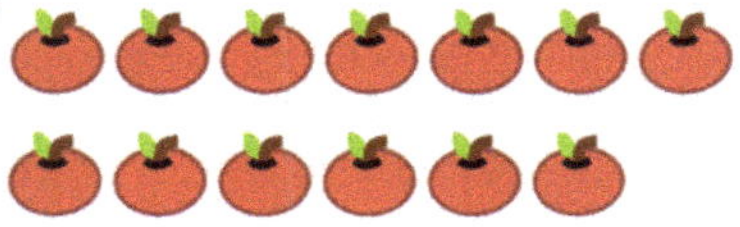

b) ___ + ___ = ___

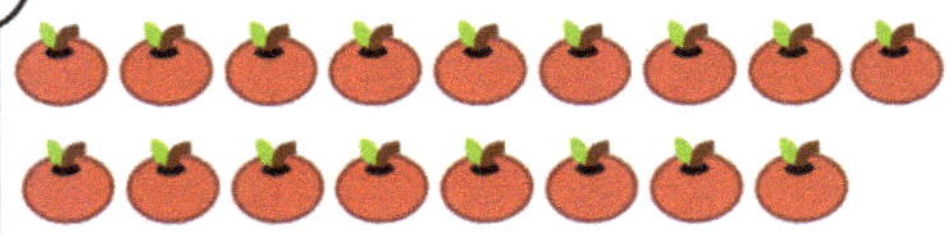

c) ___ + ___ = ___

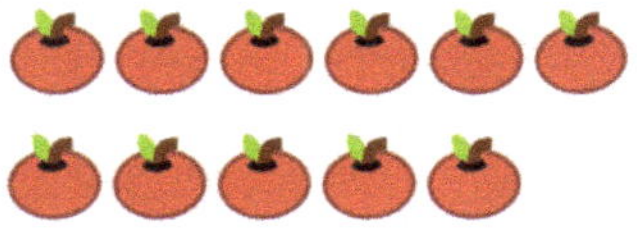

d) ___ + ___ = ___

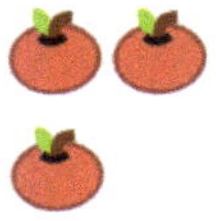

e) ___ + ___ = ___

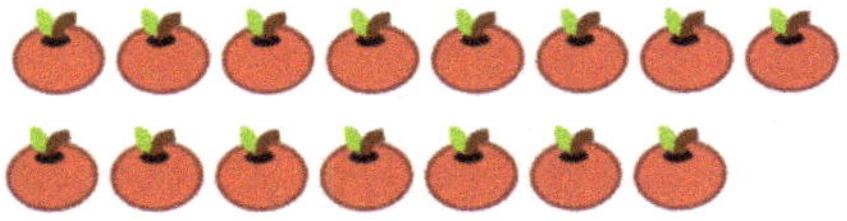

f) ___ + ___ = ___

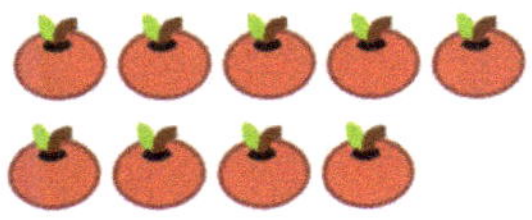

g) ___ + ___ = ___

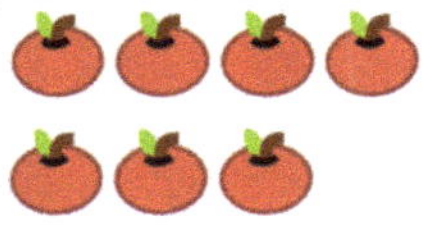

h)

1 + 1 = 2	1 + 2 = _3_	2 + 2 = 4	2 + 3 = _5_
3 + 3 = 6	3 + 4 = ___	4 + 4 = 8	4 + 5 = ___
5 + 5 = 10	5 + 6 = ___	6 + 6 = 12	6 + 7 = ___
7 + 7 = 14	7 + 8 = ___	8 + 8 = 16	8 + 9 = ___
9 + 9 = 18	9 + 10 = ___	10 + 10 = 20	

129

6. Find the buddy star for these equations:

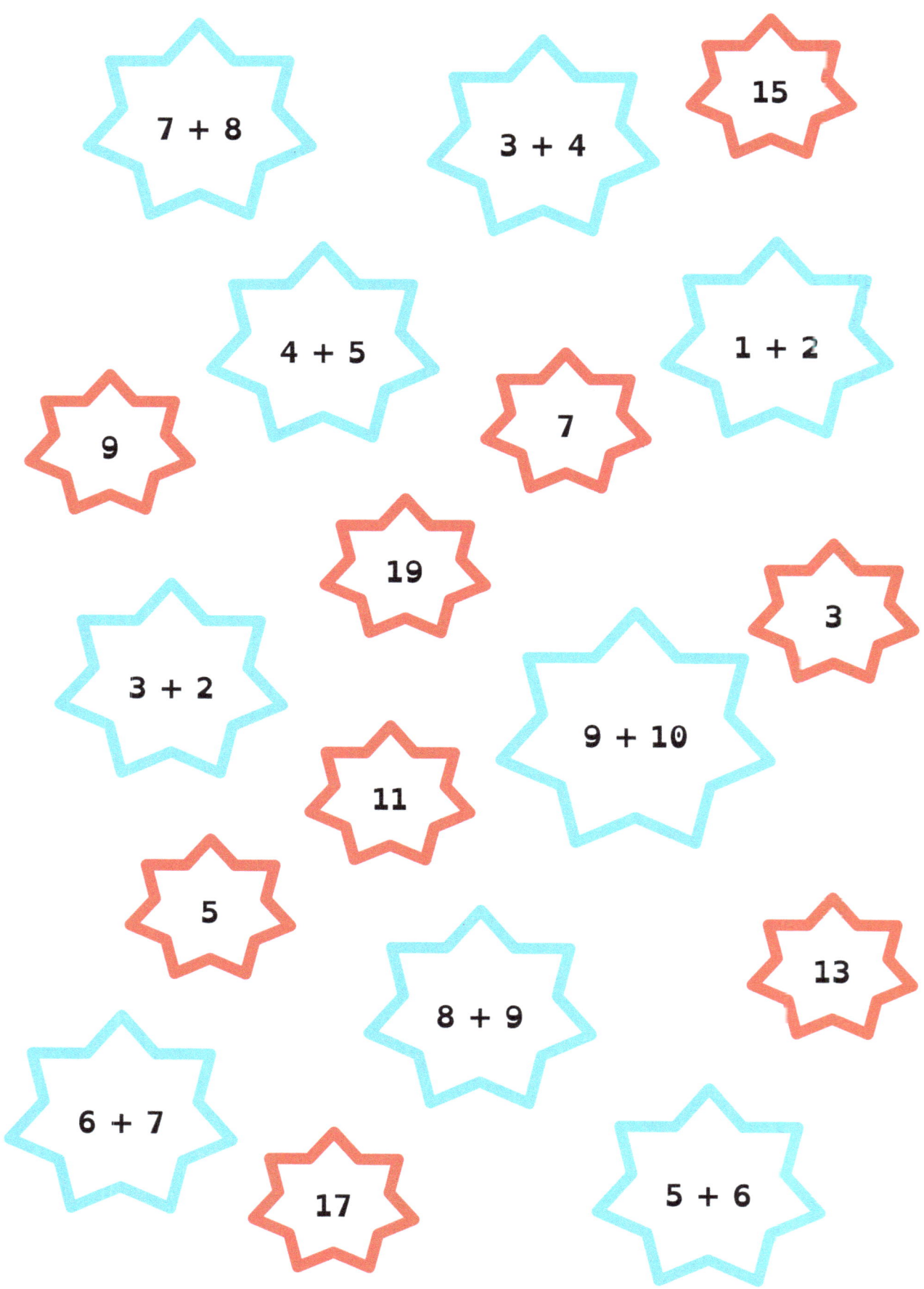

7. Now try these equations:

a)
- 2 + 3 = ____
- 5 + 5 = ____
- 2 + 1 = ____
- 5 + 4 = ____
- 7 + 6 = ____
- 9 + 10 = ____
- 4 + 3 = ____
- 8 + 9 = ____
- 8 + 7 = ____

b)
- 10 + 9 = ____
- 3 + 2 = ____
- 7 + 6 = ____
- 5 + 6 = ____
- 8 + 9 = ____
- 7 + 8 = ____
- 5 + 4 = ____
- 1 + 2 = ____
- 3 + 4 = ____

c)
- 8 + 9 = ____
- 10 + 9 = ____
- 3 + 4 = ____
- 2 + 3 = ____
- 5 + 4 = ____
- 1 + 2 = ____
- 8 + 7 = ____
- 6 + 5 = ____
- 6 + 7 = ____

d)
- 4 + 3 = ____
- 6 + 5 = ____
- 8 + 7 = ____
- 10 + 9 = ____
- 7 + 6 = ____
- 5 + 4 = ____
- 10 + 10 = ____
- 3 + 2 = ____
- 9 + 8 = ____

> **8.** Here they are all jumbled up:

a)

7 + 7 = ___	7 + 8 = ___	7 + ___ = 13
5 + 6 = ___	6 + 6 = ___	6 + ___ = 11
2 + ___ = 5	2 + 3 = ___	3 + 3 = ___

b)

9 + 9 = ___	9 + 10 = ___	9 + ___ = 10
5 + 5 = ___	5 + 4 = ___	5 + ___ = 11
4 + ___ = 7	2 + 1 = ___	8 + 9 = ___

c)

8 + 8 = ___	8 + 9 = ___	3 + ___ = 7
2 + 2 = ___	6 + ___ = 13	8 + ___ = 15
3 + ___ = 5	4 + ___ = 8	3 + ___ = 6

d)

4 + ___ = 9	7 + ___ = 15	7 + ___ = 14
6 + ___ = 13	6 + ___ = 11	6 + ___ = 12
1 + ___ = 2	5 + ___ = 9	9 + ___ = 18

9. These are the rest of the equations you want to be very familiar with. Take your time to figure them out using sums you already know (like 8 + 7 = 15 so 8 + 6 = 14).

a)
4 + 7 = _____   9 + 4 = _____   5 + 8 = _____

3 + 9 = _____   5 + 9 = _____   7 + 5 = _____

4 + 8 = _____   3 + 8 = _____   8 + 6 = _____

b)
6 + 9 = _____   4 + 7 = _____   9 + 3 = _____

4 + 8 = _____   9 + 4 = _____   5 + 9 = _____

3 + 8 = _____   5 + 8 = _____   7 + 5 = _____

c)
6 + 8 = _____   6 + 9 = _____   8 + 4 = _____

4 + 7 = _____   3 + 9 = _____   4 + 9 = _____

5 + 8 = _____   5 + 7 = _____   6 + 8 = _____

d)
6 + 9 = _____   6 + 8 = _____   5 + 7 = _____

5 + 8 = _____   8 + 3 = _____   9 + 5 = _____

9 + 4 = _____   4 + 8 = _____   3 + 9 = _____

Now we know all our basic facts, we can also use them as a tool to solve bigger equations. See the pattern in the digits here?

5 + 8 = 13

15 + 8 = 23

25 + 8 = 33

35 + 8 = 43

45 + 8 = 53

(and so on...)

85 + 8 = 93

7 + 9 = 16

17 + 9 = 26

27 + 7 = 36

37 + 9 = 46

47 + 9 = 56

(and so on...)

87 + 9 = 96

10. Use your basic facts to figure these out:

a) 26 + 8 = _____   56 + 9 = _____   88 + 4 = _____

34 + 7 = _____   43 + 9 = _____   14 + 9 = _____

55 + 8 = _____   25 + 7 = _____   36 + 8 = _____

b) 16 + 9 = _____   36 + 8 = _____   25 + 7 = _____

85 + 8 = _____   78 + 3 = _____   49 + 5 = _____

29 + 4 = _____   44 + 8 = _____   63 + 9 = _____

And just like before, your doubles and basic facts will help you with bigger numbers!

$\underline{7} + \underline{6} = \underline{13}$

$\underline{7}0 + \underline{6}0 = \underline{13}0$

$\underline{7}00 + \underline{6}00 = \underline{13}00$

etc...

$\underline{7}\,000\,000\,000 + \underline{6}\,000\,000\,000 = \underline{13}\,000\,000\,000$

Too big for a picture here!

11. Use your basic facts to help you add up these larger numbers.

a

8 + 7 = _____	5 + 9 = _____
80 + 70 = _____	50 + 90 = _____
800 + 700 = _____	500 + 900 = _____
8000 + 7000 = _____	5000 + 9000 = _____

b)

3 + 5 = _____	12 + 8 = _____
30 + 50 = _____	120 + 80 = _____
300 + 500 = _____	1200 + 800 = _____
3000 + 5000 = _____	12000 + 8000 = _____

12. Look carefully at the zeroes in each number below:

a)

7 + 2 = _____	14 + 8 = _____
70 + 20 = _____	14000 + 8000 = _____
7000 + 2000 = _____	1400 + 800 = _____
700000 + 200000 = _____	140 + 80 = _____

b)

4 + 7 = _____	13 + 3 = _____
40 + 70 = _____	130000 + 30000 = _____
8000 + 7000 = _____	1300 + 900 = _____
800000 + 700000 = _____	13000 + 9000 = _____

ANSWERS: Doubles and pairs to 20

Page 123

<u>1.</u>

a. 3   b. 3 + 3 = 6   c. 5   d. 5 + 5 = 10

e. Above, <u>Barry</u> has double the number of apples of <u>Doris.</u>

Page 124

<u>2.</u>

a. 2 + 2 = 4   b. 3 + 3 = 6   c. 4 + 4 = 8

d. 5 + 5 = 10   e. 6 + 6 = 12   f. 7 + 7 = 14

g. 8 + 8 = 16   h. 9 + 9 = 18   i. 10 + 10 = 20

Page 127 – ON NEXT PAGE

Page 128

<u>4.</u>

a.

4	10	2
8	12	18
6	16	14

b.

18	4	12
10	16	14
8	2	6

ANSWERS: Doubles and pairs to 20

Page 127

3.

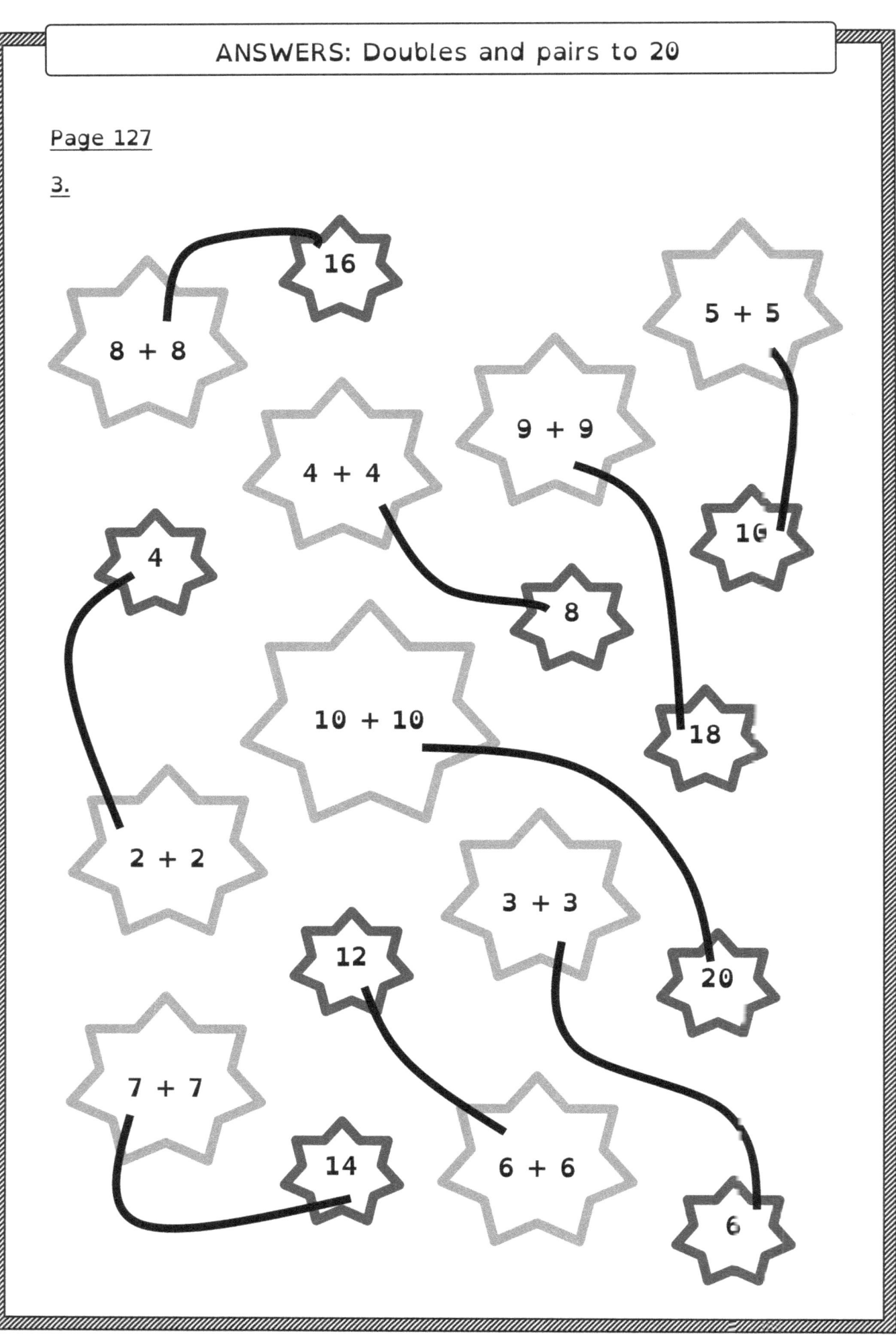

ANSWERS: Doubles and pairs to 20

Page 128

<u>4.</u>

c.
16	18	10
4	8	2
14	12	10

d.
6	10	14
18	12	8
2	4	16

Page 129

<u>5.</u>

a. 7 + 6 = 13   b. 9 + 8 = 17   c. 6 + 5 = 11

d. 2 + 1 = 3   e. 8 + 7 = 15   f. 5 + 4 = 9

g. 4 + 3 = 7

h.
1 + 1 = 2	1 + 2 = 3	2 + 2 = 4	2 + 3 = 5
3 + 3 = 6	3 + 4 = <u>7</u>	2 + 2 = 4	4 + 5 = <u>9</u>
5 + 5 = 10	5 + 6 = <u>11</u>	4 + 4 = 8	4 + 5 = <u>9</u>
7 + 7 = 14	7 + 8 = <u>15</u>	6 + 6 = 12	8 + 9 = <u>17</u>
9 + 9 = 18	9 + 10 = <u>19</u>	8 + 8 = 16	

ANSWERS: Doubles and pairs to 20

Page 130

6.

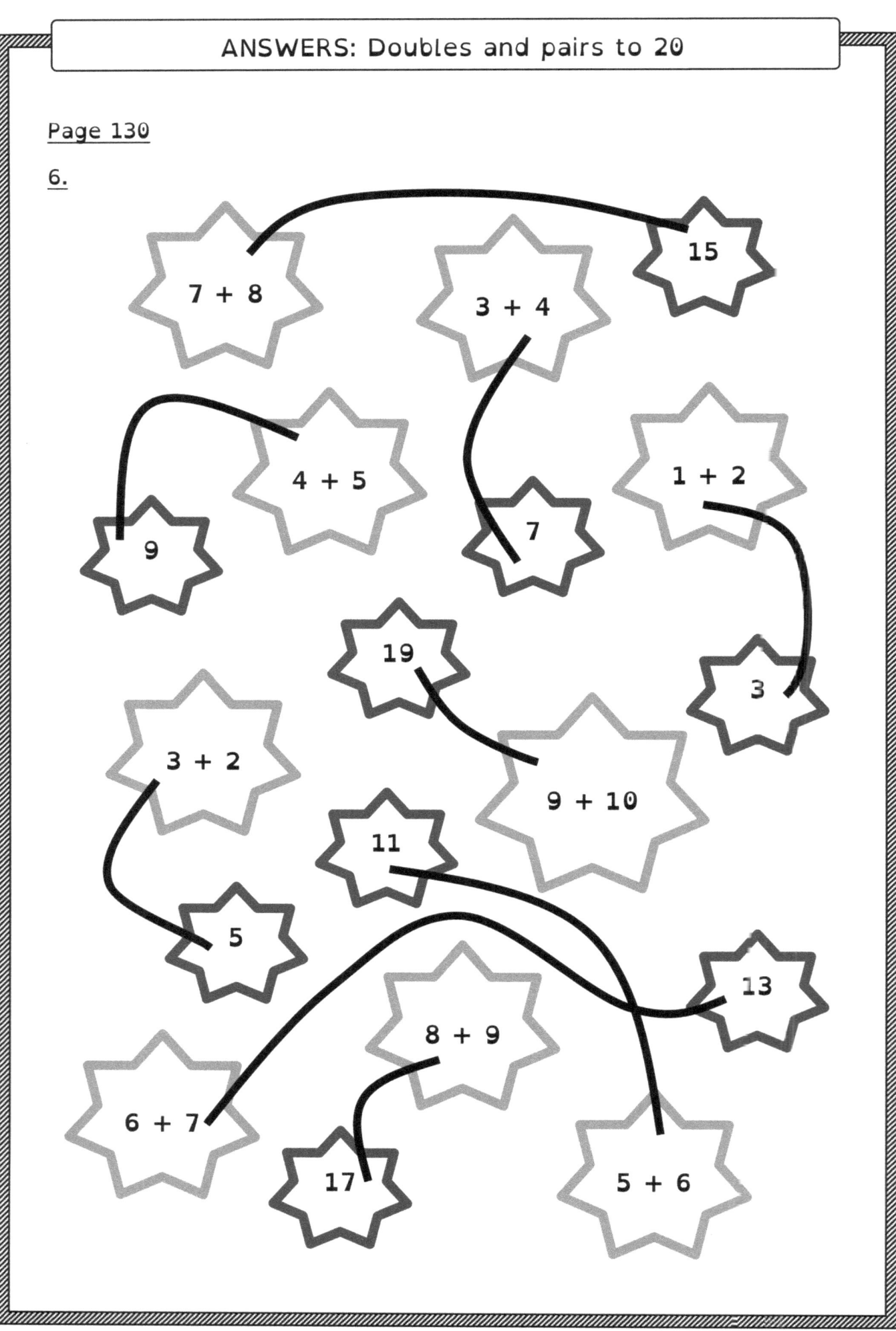

ANSWERS: Doubles and pairs to 20

Page 131

7.

a.
5	10	3
9	13	19
7	17	15

b.
19	5	13
11	17	15
9	3	7

c.
17	19	7
5	9	3
15	11	13

d.
7	11	15
19	13	9
20	5	17

ANSWERS: Doubles and pairs to 20

Page 132

<u>8.</u>

a.
14	15	6
11	12	5
3	5	6

b.
18	19	1
10	9	6
3	3	17

c.
16	17	4
4	7	7
2	4	3

d.
5	8	7
7	5	6
1	4	9

ANSWERS: Doubles and pairs to 20

Page 133

9.

a.
11	13	13
12	14	12
12	11	14

b.
15	11	12
12	13	14
11	13	12

c.
14	15	12
11	12	13
13	12	14

d.
15	14	12
13	11	14
13	12	12

ANSWERS: Doubles and pairs to 20

Page 134

10.

a.
34	65	92
41	52	23
63	32	44

b.
25	44	32
93	81	55
33	52	72

Page 135

11.

a.
15	14
150	140
1500	1400
15000	14000

Page 136

b.
8	20
80	200
800	2000
8000	20000

ANSWERS: Doubles and pairs to 20

Page 136

<u>12.</u>

a.

9	22
90	22000
9000	2200
900000	220

b.

11	16
110	160000
15000	2200
1500000	22000

Up into the hundreds

> Adding up above a hundred is very similar to what you've been doing already.

$$98 + 4 = \underline{}$$

91	92	93	94	95	96	97	98	99	100
101	102	103	104	105	106	107	108	109	110
111	112	113	114	115	116	117	118	119	120
121	122	123	124	125	126	127	128	129	130

> 1. Have a play around with this extended hundreds grid.

a) $97 + 5 = \underline{}$

b) $93 + 10 = \underline{}$

c) $96 + 12 = \underline{}$

81	82	83	84	85	86	87	88	89	90
91	92	93	94	95	96	97	98	99	100
101	102	103	104	105	106	107	108	109	110
111	112	113	114	115	116	117	118	119	120
121	122	123	124	125	126	127	128	129	130

A smooth way to do this in your head is to split a number up so you can make 100 with it. This is where pairs to 10 will come in very handy.

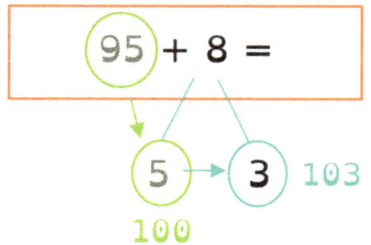

95 needs 5 more to make 100.
8 splits into 5 and 3.
95 + 5 = 100.
100 + 3 = 103.
95 + 8 = 103.

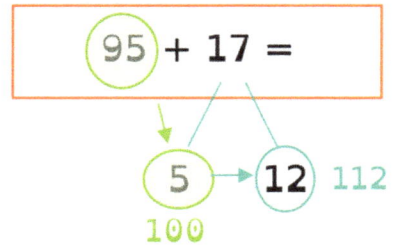

95 needs 5 more to make 100.
17 splits into 5 and 12.
95 + 5 = 100.
100 + 12 = 112.
95 + 8 = 112.

2. Use the examples above to help you solve these equations:

a
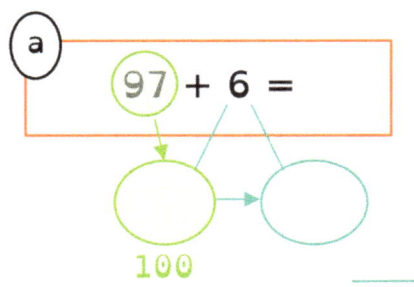

97 needs _____ more to make 100.
6 splits into _____ and _____.
97 + _____ = 100.
100 + _____ = _____.
97 + 6 = _____.

b
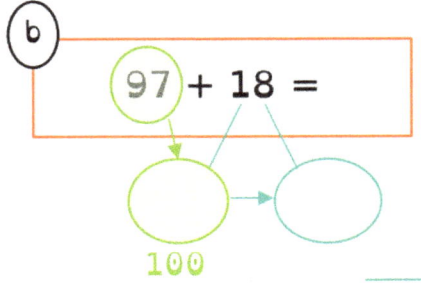

97 needs _____ more to make 100.
18 splits into _____ and _____.
97 + _____ = 100.
100 + _____ = _____.
97 + 18 = _____.

3. Here's some practice questions for you:

a
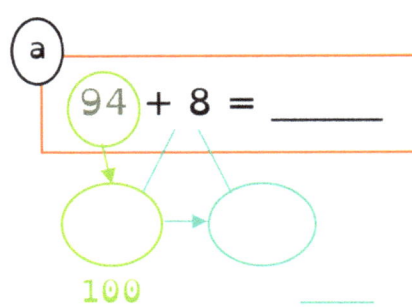

94 needs _____ more to make 100.

8 splits into _____ and _____.

94 + _____ = 100.

100 + _____ = _____.

94 + 8 = _____.

b
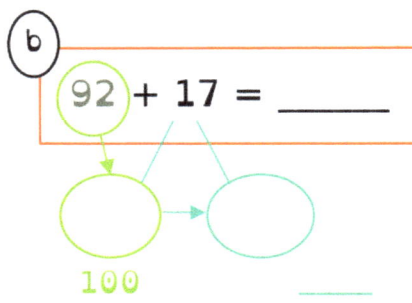

92 needs _____ more to make 100.

17 splits into _____ and _____.

92 + _____ = 100.

100 + _____ = _____.

92 + 17 = _____.

4. Use the blank working space if you need it.

a
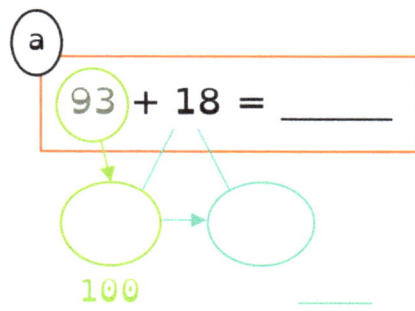

b
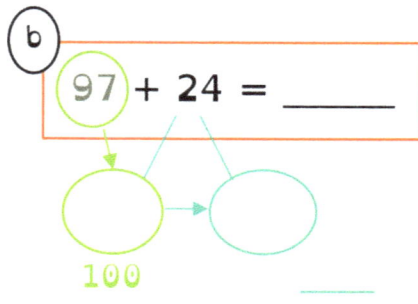

148

Adding tens into the hundreds works like this:

95 + 70 = ____

95 + 70 = 165

(9 + 7 = 16) and the 5 is added back on the end

267 + 80 = ____

267 + 80 = 347

(26 + 8 = 34) and the 7 is added back on the end

5. Have a little practice here:

a) 49 + 90 = ____

b) 82 + 50 = ____

c) 22 + 90 = ____

d) 57 + 60 = ____

e) 168 + 80 = ____

f) 177 + 70 = ____

g) 322 + 90 = ____

h) 457 + 60 = ____

6. Of course, you can also use the tidy numbers strategy too.

93 + 18 = _____
20 → −2

93 + 20 = 113.
113 − 2 = 111.

93 + 18 = 111.

97 + 24 = ____
20 → +4

97 + ____ = ____.

____ + ____ = ____.

97 + 24 = _____.

7. Try both strategies out and see which one you prefer (it may also change depending on the question). We won't spend too long on this since there's more (and better) strategies to come later.

a) 95 + 19 = ____

b) 98 + 33 = ____

These are some things to watch out for. Equations can become sneaky when they're next to their friends, but as long as you take notice of the place value of the numbers, you'll be fine.

36 + 6 = 42   vs.   36 + 60 = 96

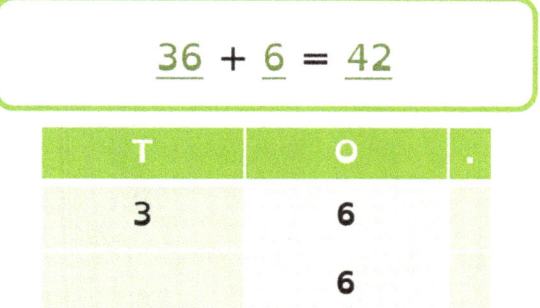

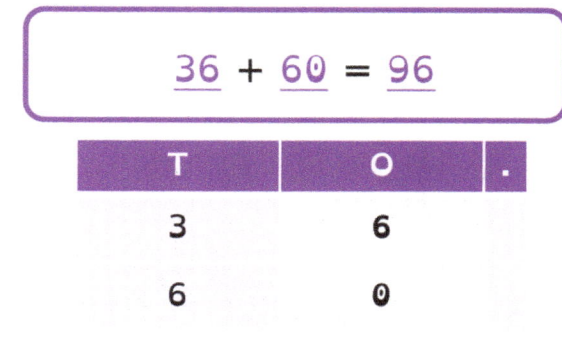

36 + 6 =
6 + 6 = 12
so 36 + 6 = 42

36 + 60 =
30 + 60 = 90
so 36 + 60 = 96

Here are some other examples of how we can have different place value positions (these are the above equations multiplied by 10):

360 + 60 = 420

360 + 600 = 960

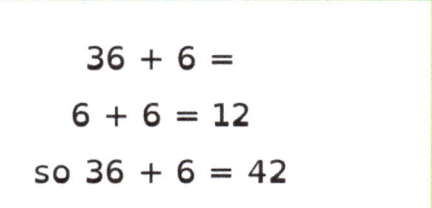

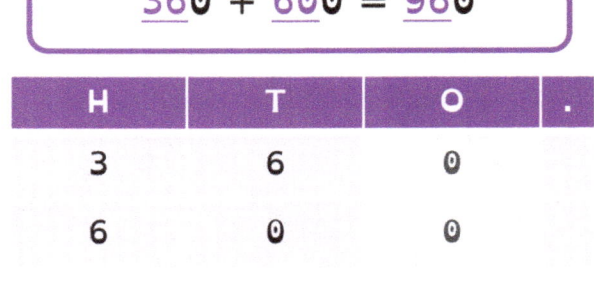

Drop the end 0 for now and look at it like 36 + 6.
36 + 6 = 42
Add 0 back: 360 + 60 = 420

Drop the end 0 for now and look at it like 36 + 60.
36 + 60 = 96.
Add 0 back: 360 + 600 = 960

The way we line numbers up makes a difference to what answer we will get. Take close notice of the number of zeroes in each number.

$3\underline{6}00 + \underline{6}00 = \underline{42}00$

Th	H	T	O	.
3	6	0	0	
	6	0	0	

Drop the two end 0s for now, look at it like 36 + 6.
36 + 6 = 42
Add 0s back: 3600 + 600 = 4200

$36\underline{0} + \underline{6} = 36\underline{6}$

H	T	O	.
3	6	0	
		6	

Notice 6 is in the ones column 360 has 0 in the ones column.
0 + 6 = 6, so 360 + 6 = 366

8. Here's your chance to practise this. Solve these equations.

a

2 + 3 = _____

20 + 3 = _____

250 + 30 = _____

2500 + 300 = _____

250 + 300 = _____

20 + 30 = _____

2 + 30 = _____

25 + 30 = _____

2500 + 30 = _____

250000 + 300000 = _____

b

27 + 9 = _____

2700 + 900 = _____

35 + 8 = _____

35 + 80 = _____

3500 + 80 = _____

350 + 8000 = _____

36 + 60 = _____

36 + 6 = _____

360 + 60 = _____

36000 + 60000 = _____

570 + 90 = _____

570000 + 9000 = _____

ANSWERS: Up into the hundreds

Page 146

__1.__

a. 102   b. 103   c. 118

Page 147

__2.__

a. 97 needs 3 more to make 100. 6 splits into 3 and 3. 97 + 3 = 100. 100 + 3 = 103. 97 + 6 = 103.

b. 97 needs 3 more to make 100. 18 splits into 3 and 15. 97 + 3 = 100. 100 + 15 = 115. 97 + 18 = 115.

Page 148

__3.__

a. 94 needs 6 more to make 100. 8 splits into 6 and 2. 94 + 6 = 100. 100 + 2 = 102. 94 + 8 = 102.

b. 92 needs 8 more to make 100. 17 splits into 8 and 9. 92 + 8 = 100. 100 + 9 = 109. 92 + 17 = 109.

__4.__

a. 93 needs 7 more to make 100. 18 splits into 7 and 11. 93 + 7 = 100. 100 + 11 = 111. 93 + 18 = 111.

b. 97 needs 3 more to make 100. 24 splits into 3 and 21. 97 + 3 = 100. 100 + 21 = 121. 97 + 24 = 121.

ANSWERS: Up into the hundreds

Page 149

<u>5.</u>

a. 139   b. 132

c. 112   d. 117

e. 248   f. 247

g. 412   h. 517

Page 150

<u>6.</u> 97 + <u>20</u> = <u>117</u>. <u>117</u> + <u>4</u> = <u>121</u>. 97 + 24 = <u>121</u>.

<u>7.</u>

a.

Option 1 (tidy numbers)

19 is close to 20. 20 − 1 = 19.

95 + 20 = 115, 115 − 1 = 114. 95 + 19 = 114.

Option 2 (split to make 100 first)

95 needs 5 more to make 100. 19 splits into 5 and 14.

95 + 5 = 100. 100 + 14 = 114. 95 + 19 = 114

b.

Option 1 (tidy numbers)

33 is close to 30. 30 + 3 = 33.

98 + 30 = 128. 128 + 3 = 131. 98 + 33 = 131.

Option 2 (split to make 100 first)

98 needs 2 more to make 100. 33 splits into 2 and 31.

98 + 2 = 100. 100 + 31 = 131. 98 + 33 = 131.

ANSWERS: Up into the hundreds

Page 152

8.

a.
5	50
23	32
280	55
2800	2530
550	550000

b.
36	96
3600	96
43	960
115	96000
3580	660
8350	579000

A final review

1. Here's a review of what you've learnt so far. Look how far you've come!

a

33 + 9 = _____	330 + 90 = _____
26 + 8 = _____	260 + 80 = _____
48 + 9 = _____	480 + 90 = _____
72 + 6 = _____	720 + 60 = _____
33 + 5 = _____	3300 + 500 = _____

b

29 + 9 = _____	290 + 900 = _____
78 + 4 = _____	780 + 4 = _____
63 + 7 = _____	630 + 70 = _____
136 + 8 = _____	136 + 80 = _____
180 + 30 = _____	1800 + 300 = _____

c

55 + 5 = _____	55 + 500 = _____
87 + 9 = _____	90 + 87 = _____
380 + 60 = _____	3800 + 6000 = _____
4200 + 7000 = _____	4200 + 700 = _____
4200 + 70 = _____	4200 + 7 = _____

2. You're now ready for the next stage of your adventure in the wild world of math out there. See how powerfully you defeat all these questions?

a
- 3 + 8 = _____
- 30 + 80 = _____
- 20 + _____ = 100
- 200 + _____ = 1000
- 4 + 5 = _____
- 40000 + 50000 = _____

b
- 7 + 8 = _____
- 700 + 800 = _____
- 300 + 900 = _____
- 30000 + 90000 = _____
- 4 + _____ = 10
- 400000 + _____ = 1000000
- 20 + 10 = _____
- 2000 + 1000 = _____

c
- 60 + 80 = _____
- 60000 + 80000 = _____
- 7000 + 4000 = _____
- 70000 + 40000 = _____
- 30 + _____ = 100
- 3000 + _____ = 10000
- 5 + 9 = _____
- 50000 + 90000 = _____

d
- 1 + 9 = _____
- 100 + 900 = _____
- 200 + 700 = _____
- 2000 + 7000 = _____
- 90 + _____ = 100
- 900 + _____ = 1000
- 20 + 20 = _____
- 200000 + 200000 = _____

157

3. Once these questions have been conquered, you will be fully equipped for Book 2!

a

a + a = _____   2a + 2a = _____

a + a + a = _____   3a + 2b + 4a = _____

a + a + b = _____   7b + 9b = _____

a + a + b + b + b = _____   700a + 900a = _____

b

2 + _____ = 10   3a + _____ = 10a

2a + _____ = 10a   50a + _____ = 100a

200a + _____ = 1000a   800a + _____ = 1000a

20000a + _____ = 100000a   60a + _____ = 100a

c

25 + _____ = 100   46 + _____ = 100

$25x$ + _____ = $100x$ $460y$ + _____ = $1000y$

37 + _____ = 100   59 + _____ = 100

$3700x$ + _____ = $10000x$ $5900y$ + _____ = $10000y$

d

15 + _____ = 60   41 + _____ = 70

37a + _____ = 80a $63x$ + _____ = $90x$

22 + _____ = 40   34 + _____ = 50

$84x$ + _____ = $100x$ 28a + _____ = 80a

Bonus: Solve the word problems!

1. Welcome back to the word problems you encountered before. Here are questions you now have the skills to solve. Give them your best shot!

a) You have already saved $5 and then you save another $4 this week.

How much money do you have in total?

This question is asking:

_____ + _____ = _____

b) You have 8 carrots in your fridge at home, and you buy another 4 at the market.

How many carrots do you have in total?

This question is asking:

_____ + _____ = _____

c) You have $60 in your savings and then you save another $72 this week.

How much money do you have in total?

This question is asking:

_____ + _____ =

Working space:

Answer: _____

d

You're going on a trip to the beach. Your first bus ticket will cost you $8, and then your second bus ticket will cost you $9. How much will your bus tickets cost you in total?

This question is asking:

_____ + _____ = _____

e

You saved $25 last week, and then $35 this week. How much did you save in total over the two weeks?

This question is asking:

_____ + _____ = _____

f

A carrot farmer is trying to break the world record for the world's biggest carrot. Last week, he planted 38 giant carrot seeds. This week, he planted 29 more.
How many giant carrots did he plant in total?

This question is asking:

_____ + _____ =

Working space:

Answer: _____

2. These next questions are a bit more challenging, but you could figure them out using strategies we've learnt. If you get stuck, we'll learn more strategies in Book 2 that helps especially with large equations.

a) You're going on holiday. Your first plane ticket will cost you $450, and then your second plane ticket will cost you $360.

How much will your plane tickets cost you in total?

This question is asking:

_____ + _____ =

Working space:

Answer: _____

b) You make and sell carrot cakes for a living. You have 700 carrots in your fridge at work, and you buy another 690 at the market.

How many carrots do you have in total?

This question is asking:

_____ + _____ =

Working space:

Answer: _____

c At the start of your month your savings is $2400. After the first fortnight* you save $500 more, and then during the second fortnight you save $600 more. (*A fortnight is 2 weeks.)

How much do you have saved at the end of the month?

This question is asking:

_____ + _____ + _____ =

Working space:

Answer: _____

d You're going on a tropical holiday. Your accommodation costs $4320, and your plane tickets cost $870.

How much will this holiday cost you in total?

This question is asking:

_____ + _____ =

Working space:

Answer: _____

ANSWERS: A final review

Page 156

1.

a.
42	420
34	340
57	570
78	780
38	3800

b.
38	1190
82	784
90	700
144	216
210	2100

c.
60	555
96	177
44	9800
11200	4900
4270	4207

ANSWERS: A final review

Page 157:

2.

a.
11	110
80	800
9	90000

b.
15	1500
1200	120000
6	600000
30	3000

c.
140	140000
11000	110000
70	7000
14	140000

d.
10	1000
900	9000
10	100
40	400000

ANSWERS: A final review

Page 158

3.

a.
2a	4a
3a	7a + 2b
2a + b	16b
2a + 3b	1600a

b.
8	7a
8a	50a
800a	200a
80000a	40a

c.
75	54
$75x$	$540y$
63	41
$6300x$	$4100y$

d.
45	29
43a	$27x$
18	16
$16x$	53a

ANSWERS:

Bonus: Solve the word problems!

Page 159

<u>1.</u>

a. 5 + 4 = $9

b. 8 + 4 = 12

c. 60 + 72 = $132

Page 160

d. 8 + 9 = $17

e. 25 + 35 = $60

f. 38 + 29 = 67

Page 161

<u>2.</u> (You may have picked different strategies. These are here for if you get stuck.)

a. 450 + 360 = $810

    First do 45 + 36.

    45 + 6 = 51, so 45 + 36 = 81.

    Then put the 0 back on the end to make it 810

b. 700 + 690 = 1390

      690 is close to 700. 700 − 10 = 690.

      700 + 700 = 1400. 1400 − 10 = 1390.

ANSWERS:
Bonus: Solve the word problems!

Page 162

<u>2.</u>

c. 2400 + 500 + 600 = $3500

It's easiest to first add 2400 + 600, which equals 3000. Then add 500 which equals 3500.

d. 4320 + 870 = $5190

870 is close to 900. 900 − 30 = 870,

4320 + 900 = 5220 (4320 + 1000 − 100 = 5220)

5220 − 30 = 5190

Congratulations on finishing Book 1 of Number, Addition and Place Value!

I hope you and numbers are starting to become good friends.

What is a reader-friendly font?

We use OpenDyslexia font because we love fonts that all readers are able to read and which are especially designed to help those with dyslexia. Many children are undiagnosed, have other difficulties with reading, or very ashamed at being called dyslexic so we use the same font for all children. We also love the way it looks!

This typeface does the following:

1. The letters are weighted on the bottom to show direction and stop the brain rotating them (e.g., stops a p looking like a b).

2. Each letter has a unique shape which can help stop the brain from

- flipping letters (e.g., stops a b looking like a d).

- swapping letters (e.g., stops the capital letter I looking like a .ower-case letter L, e.g., in Gill Sans I vs l).

- swapping letters for numbers (e.g., stops the number one looking like the lower-case letter L, e.g., in Times New Roman: 1 vs l)

3. Increasing spacing between letters so they don't run into each other (e.g., stops the two letters rn from looking like m, e.g., in Times New Roman rn vs m)

Gill Sans	rn m	MW	dpqb	lI lijJ
Verdana	rn m	MW	dpqb	l1IijJ
OpenDyslexic	rn m	MW	dpqb	l1IijJ
Times	rn m	MW	dpqb	l1IijJ
Helvetica	rn m	MW	dpqb	l1IijJ

www.ingramcontent.com/pod-product-compliance
Lightning Source LLC
Chambersburg PA
CBHW042015090526
44587CB00027B/4266